BARRIERS *of* LEADERSHIP

"For the Kenyan immigrants to succeed in seeking and attaining leadership positions in the U.S., it is important that they adopt leadership styles or behaviors that are acceptable within the American culture. "

Dr. John Onuko Mobegi

EXPLORING BARRIERS KENYAN IMMIGRANTS FACE IN ATTAINING LEADERSHIP POSITIONS IN NORTHERN CALIFORNIA: A PHENOMENOLOGICAL STUDY

BY

DR. JOHN ONUKO MOBEGI

STUDY SUPERVISION

OGWO UMEH, PHD

BETHANY MICKAHAIL, PHD

GHOLAM ALI SHAYKHIAN, PHD

School of Advanced Studies
University of Phoenix

American Journal of
Transformational Leadership

ProQuest Dissertations
ProQuest Databases

Texas International
Guardian, Inc.

John Onuko Mobegi © 2016 All rights reserved.
CreateSpace Independent Publishing Platform.
ISBN-13: 978-1546756682
ISBN-10: 154675668X
Printed in the United States of America (USA).

Cover design and book design *by Dr. Anthony Obi Ogbo,*
Production *by International Guardian*
Publishing: *American Journal of Transformational Leadership*

This book is a reproduction of studies based on a Dissertation presented by
John Onuko Mobegi in partial fulfillment of the requirements for the degree
Doctor of Management in Organizational Leadership

Research Study Supervision
Ogwo Umeh, PhD
Bethany Mickahail, PhD
Gholam Ali Shaykhian, PhD

Research Study Approval
William C. Beck II, PhD
Academic Dean, School of Advanced Studies,
University of Phoenix

DEDICATION

I would like to dedicate the dissertation to my late grandfather Patroba Onuko and my late grandmother Priscilla Nyantune. Thank you for blessing me with the courage, the wisdom, and the determination to do anything in life. Thank you for listening and offering kind words of encouragement. Your words of wisdom and compassion kept me grounded. You are the wind beneath my wings. The personal sacrifices made during your lifetime are greatly appreciated, and I know you are proud and smiling down on me each day. Thank you.

Special dedication goes to my uncle Sospeter Mageto and Aunt Eleanor Moraa. Thank you for the support, love, guidance, words of encouragement and the opportunity to move forward in life. Your belief in me gave me wings to fly. I also dedicate the dissertation to all of my family members and those who helped and supported my academic endeavors over the years.

APPRECIATION

I want to acknowledge, give praise and glory to God for with Him all things are possible in life. I want to thank my Mum, my wife Angela and our children – Elijah, Shem, Zaidi and Taji. Thank you for the sacrifices you made and allowed me the time to study and complete my educational goal. Thank you all for the love, support, and under-standing during my doctoral journey. You made it easier for me to pursue my dream and for that I am grateful. I would like to thank Dorothy and Michael Thornton for letting me stay at their house while attending residence in Phoenix.

Thank you to all of the helpful individuals who participated in this dissertation. I appreciate your time devoted to helping me along my doctoral journey. I am forever grateful for your assistance.

Lastly, I was privileged and grateful to have Dr. Ogwo Umeh as my mentor and committee chair. Dr. Umeh, thank you for the conversa-tions, feedbacks, your dedication, professional guidance, support and encouragement that provided the motivation I needed to remain fo-cused on completing my doctoral journey. To my committee team members, Dr. Bethany Mickahail, and Dr. Gholam Ali Shaykhian, thank you for the valuable feedbacks and support during my doctoral dissertation journey. There were many challenges, but you helped me through them. Thank You.

ABSTRACT

The United States of America was founded by immigrants who came in search of opportunities and religious freedom. The Kenyan immigrants migrated to the United States to seek for education and employment opportunities. As immigrants arrive in the United States, they are faced with complex challenges that include cultural, social, political, and economical barriers. The goal of this qualitative and phenomenological research study was to explore the problem of barriers immigrants' face in attaining leadership positions in private and public organizations in the United States. This study was guided by one research question: How do Kenyan immigrants in mid to senior management positions perceive and describe their experiences on barriers in attaining leadership positions? The study participants were 20 Kenyan immigrants who were holding mid to senior management positions in their respective organizations in Northern California. The data for this study was subjected to an analysis using the seven steps of Van Kaam's method, developed by Hursell and modified by Moustakas, and NVivo 11 computer software to identify themes through data coding and distillation. The themes that emerged were: (a) networking, (b) social environment, (c) leadership process, (d) culture, (e), economic environment, (f) organization politics, and (g) discrimination. The study results might provide the Kenyan immigrants with important information to better understand the steps to take and the pitfalls to avoid in attaining leadership positions. Organizations and policy makers may use the findings as a tool to identify the barriers working against immigrants' career advancement and direct corrective measures to relevant areas.

TABLE OF CONTENTS

III ▪ Chapter 3: Research Methods

TABLE OF CONTENTS

TABLE OF CONTENTS

V ▪ Chapter 5: Conclusions and Recommendations

LIST OF TABLES

LIST OF FIGURES

Chapter 1
Introduction

In the study, the Kenyan immigrants in mid to senior management positions had the opportunity to provide a description of their lived experiences and perceptions on barriers to advancing to leadership positions,

The Migration Policy Institute (MPI) reported that the number of Kenyan-born immigrants in the United States had continued to grow rapidly for the last two decades (MPI, 2015). The number of Kenyan immigrants who lived in the United States (U.S.) in 2010 as per the Immigration Policy Center (IPC) was 88,519 (IPC, 2012). The Kenyan immigrants were spread across the United States, but the majority lived in states such as Minnesota, Washington State, New York, Georgia, Washington D.C., Massachusetts, Texas and California (MPI, 2015). The largest population of Kenyan immigrants lived in Texas and California with a population of about 10, 000 each (MPI, 2015).

The MPI (2015) report indicated that the Kenyan immigrants in the United States age 16 and above were in the labor force, and 93 percent of these immigrants in the U.S. labor force were employed. The Kenyan immigrants were also in more professional or management occupations than the U.S. general public. The occupations Kenyan immigrants were involved include specialized fields such as engineering, science, law or education (MPI, 2015). They were also involved in administrative and managerial jobs such as finance or human resources (MPI, 2015). MPI (2015) also reported that some Kenyan immigrants working as registered nurses or nurse's aides were 10% and 17 % respectively. Of all these occupations Kenyan immigrants were involved in, there was no evidence of any Kenyan immigrants as leaders or chief executive officers (CEO) in any organization (MPI, 2015). There was no convincing explanation as to why considering 93 percent of Kenyan immigrants in the U.S. labor force were employed but were not represented in executive leadership positions (MPI, 2015).

The research efforts to find out the lived experiences and perceptions of Kenyan immigrants in leadership positions in the United States remained limited (MPI, 2015). As a result, this study was used to explore the cultural, social, political, and economic barriers perceived to be preventing Kenyan immigrants in mid to senior management positions from attaining leadership positions in the United States with a concentration in Northern California. Wamwara-Mbugua and Cornwell (2010) argued that some of the barriers Kenyan immigrants were faced with upon migrating included difficulty in assimilating into the American culture (acculturation process), language or communication barrier, racial stratification, marginalization, and education (Berry, 2003; Shinnar, 2007).

The Kenyan immigrants, in particular, had difficulty in making adjustments to the new environment in the U.S., and the adaptation process was affected by their race and former colonial backgrounds (Gilmore & Miller, 2013; Wamwara-Mbugua & Cornwell, 2010). The majority of Kenyan immigrants have a good command of the English language considering the country was under the British colonial rule, but the accent was an impediment because it communicated to some that persons with an accent were uninformed and unintelligent (Ande, 2009; McCabe, 2011; Wamwara-Mbugua, Cornwell, & Boller, 2006; Wamwara-Mbugua & Cornwell, 2010). Wamwara-Mbugua and Cornwell (2010) posited that immigrants came to the United States unaware of racial classification, but they had to assimilate as members of different racial groups in the country. Racial stratification shaped the life of all black people in the United States, and Kenyan immigrants were not exempt (Gilmore & Miller, 2013; Wamwara-Mbugua, Cornwell, & Boller, 2006).

The population for this study consisted of Kenyan immigrants residing in Northern California. Northern California was structurally diverse with Kenyan immigrants from different geopolitical regions. Through a qualitative phenomenological method and empirical phenomenological research design, this study was used to explore in depth the insights and lived experiences of 20 Kenyan immigrants in regards to the barriers in attaining leadership positions phenomenon. The study focused on Kenyan immigrants who occupied mid to senior level management positions in their organizations. This group of Kenyan immigrants shared their experiences and perceptions on cultural, social, political, and economic barriers they perceived prevented them from advancing to leadership positions in their respective organizations in Northern California.

The preceding discussion was used to introduce the problem of barriers Kenyan immigrants faced in attaining leadership positions in Northern California. Included in Chapter 1 was the background of the problem under review, problem statement, the purpose of this study, the significance of this study, and nature of this study. The research question that guided this study was stated, and the theoretical framework was discussed in detail. The discussion in this chapter also included definitions of terms used in the study, assumptions, scope, the limitations, the delimitations, and a summary of issues discussed.

Background of the Problem

According to the American Community Survey (ACS) briefs, approximately 39.8 million foreign-born people also known as immigrants were residing in the United States from 2008 to 2012, this included 1.6 million people coming from the continent of Africa, which represented 4 percent of the total immigrants (Gambino, Trevelyan, & Fitzwater, 2014; U.S. Census Bureau, 2014; Yonghee Suh, Sohyun, & Forest, 2015). The ACS survey showed that African-Born immigrants in the United States doubled every decade since 1970 and the largest increase occurred from 2008 to 2012 (U.S. Census Bureau, 2014). The ACS report indicated that African-born population grew from 80,000 in 1970 to about 1.6 million during the period from 2008 to 2012 (Gambino, Trevelyan, & Fitzwater, 2014).

After World War II, there was a sharp increase in migration from the continent of Africa, as immigrants responded to the need for education and employment opportunities abroad (Arthur, 2000; Takougang & Tidjani, 2009). After World War II, most Africans migrated to other countries in Africa and former European colonial masters until placement of restrictions on immigration in Western Europe (Gordon, 1998). Migration from the continent of Africa to the U.S. increased after the national origin quota system was replaced by Immigration Act of 1965, which had favored immigrants from Europe with a new law that prioritized skilled labor, uniting separated families, and migration based on humanitarian grounds (Berlin, 2010; Gambino, Trevelyan, & Fitzwater, 2014; Jaggers, Gabbard, & Jaggers, 2014; U.S. Department of State, 2015).

The American Community Survey report revealed that about a quarter of immigrants from the continent of Africa to the U.S. in the year 2010, entered as refugees or received asylum due to ethnic conflict in their home countries, or civil war in their countries such as Sudan, Somalia, and Liberia to name a few (Capps, McCabe & Fix, 2012; Gambino, Trevelyan & Fitzwater, 2014; McCabe, 2011). The rate of immigrants coming from Africa and living in the United States continue to go up as immigrants network grow and pathways are established (Arthur, 2010; Gambino, Trevelyan, & Fitzwater, 2014; McCabe, 2011; Takougang & Tidjani,

2009).

Based on ACS report, of the 1.6 million African-born immigrants in the United States, 36 percent were from West African countries, 29 percent from East African countries, 17 percent from North African countries, 5 percent from South African countries, 5 percent from Central African countries, and 7 percent came from other African countries (Gambino, Trevelyan, & Fitzwater, 2014). Countries from Africa with the largest African-born immigrants in the United States were Nigeria and Ghana in West Africa; Ethiopia, Kenya, and Somalia from East Africa; Egypt in North Africa; and South Africa from southern part of Africa (Gambino, Trevelyan, & Fitzwater, 2014; McCabe, 2011; U.S. Census Bureau, 2014). The top five countries with the most African immigrants in the United States as per the Immigration Policy Center report in 2010 was from Nigerian (219,309), Ethiopia (173,592), Egypt (137,799), Ghana (124,696), and Kenya (88,519) (IPC, 2012).

The Migration Policy Institute report posited that the population of Kenyan-born immigrants in the United States had grown rapidly in the last two decades (MPI, 2015). The United States was ranked second as the country of destination for most Kenyan immigrants due to the yearly Diversity Visa program which benefits migrant populations with a small presence in the U.S. (Johnson, 2014; Kioko, 2010; MPI, 2015; U.S. Department of State, 2015). The Kenyan immigrants are found in most states across the country. The largest population of Kenyan immigrants lived in Texas and California with a population of about 10, 000 each (MPI, 2015).

Like any other immigrants, Kenyans encountered huge challenges and barriers in their quest for success in the United

States (Gilmore & Miller, 2013; Kioko, 2010). The challenges facing minorities especially the African-American in
the United States were also experienced by immigrants from
Africa that included immigrants from Kenya (Wamwara-
Mbugua, Cornwell, & Boller, 2006; Wamwara-Mbugua &
Cornwell, 2010). The Kenyan diaspora population in the
United States was well educated, involved in professional or
managerial occupations and had a high percentage of the
labor force but continued to be underrepresented in top leadership positions (MPI, 2015).

Problem Statement
 The general problem that was addressed in this study was
barriers immigrants' faced in attaining leadership positions in
private and public organizations in the United States.
Jimenez (2011) posited that when immigrants first arrived
and settled in the United States, they were faced with some
natural barriers to full social, economic and political participation. But over time, the gap between immigrants and the
rest of society narrowed as they interacted with members of
the host country and became actively involved in participating in the political process. The integration progress of different immigrant groups in the United States remained
uneven (Rumano, 2009). The process of full integration into
the U.S. society, Jimenez (2011) argued, took more than one
generation. This meant that the first generation of Kenyan
immigrants faced significant difficulties in becoming fully in-
tegrated into the U.S. society (Gilmore & Miller, 2013).
 The specific problem or barriers Kenyan immigrants in
mid to senior management positions faced in attaining leadership positions in private and public organizations in Northern

California was explored. According to the Immigration Policy Institute report, the state of California had one of the largest populations of Kenyan immigrants with a population of about 10,000 immigrants (MPI, 2015). The exact number of Kenyan immigrants residing in Northern California was not known, and research efforts to find out was limited perhaps due to the comparatively insignificant number of Kenyan immigrants coming to this region (Baker & Rytina, 2014; Rumano, 2009). There existed a need to bridge the knowledge gap on the lived experiences and perceptions of barriers Kenyan immigrants perceived prevented them from attaining leadership positions in Northern California.

Using a qualitative research method and a phenomenological research design the goal of the present study was to explore lived experiences and perceptions of barriers Kenyan immigrants in mid to senior management positions faced in attaining leadership positions in private and public organizations in Northern California. Data collection involved face-to-face interviews, digital recording of interviews, notes taking, and observing 20 Kenyan immigrants purposefully selected from the Kenyan community of immigrants who were residing in Northern California. Using the seven steps of Van Kaam's method, developed by Hursell and modified by Moustakas (Moustakas, 1994), and NVivo 11 computer software for analysis (QSR International, 2016), transcribed data was coded and analyzed for themes.

In the study, the Kenyan immigrants in mid to senior management positions had the opportunity to provide a description of their lived experiences and perceptions on barriers to advancing to leadership positions, and as a result, "shedding more light on the subject of investigation" (Moustakas, 1994,

p. 58). The results of this study may be useful to policy makers in various institutions and various organizational leaders to identify growth barriers for immigrants and find ways to overcome them. The results of this study may create awareness to future Kenyan immigrants or immigrants from other countries who aspire to succeed in attaining leadership positions in the United States on what to expect and possibly find ways to overcome them.

Purpose of the Study

The purpose statement is used to identify the objective, the intent, and the major idea or reason for a research study (Leedy & Ormrod, 2010). The purpose of this qualitative phenomenological research study was to explore the lived experiences and perceptions of Kenyan immigrants in mid to senior management positions to better understand barriers impeding promotion opportunities to leadership positions in Northern California. The focus of the current study was on Kenyan immigrants who occupied mid to senior level management positions in their respective industries. This group of immigrants shared their experiences and perceptions of barriers they were confronted with in attaining leadership positions in private and public organizations in Northern California.

Participants for the study were selected from Kenyan immigrants residing in Northern California. To collect the data, open-ended interview questions were used to elicit the Kenyan immigrants' experiences and perceptions regarding barriers they experienced in attaining leadership positions in their respective fields. In this study, a qualitative research method and interpretive phenomenological research design were used to describe, understand, and interpret participants' experiences (Tuohy, Cooney, Dowling, Murphy, & Sixsmith, 2013).

The seven steps of Van Kaam's method, developed by Hursell and modified by Moustakas (Moustakas, 1994), was used to analyze data for the current study. Van Kaam's method provided a systematic process to analyze the collected data. The resulting themes assisted in understanding the barriers Kenyan immigrants faced in attaining leadership positions in Northern California. A pilot study using two participants was conducted prior to the actual interview to ensure interview questions gathered the information that was needed to achieve the objective of this study, and that the interview process was successful (Chenail, 2011).

Significance of the Study

The current study was significant because it examined the barriers Kenyan immigrants faced in attaining leadership positions from the perspective of those who were already in mid to senior level management positions in various organizations in Northern California. The findings from this study may be beneficial to policy makers in various institutions and organizational leaders to identify growth barriers for immigrants and find ways to bridge the gap (Takougang & Tidjani, 2009). The findings of the study may also become beneficial to future Kenyan immigrants or immigrants from other countries who aspire to succeed in attaining leadership positions in the United States to be aware of and prepare for the challenges and plan accordingly (Baker & Rytina, 2014).

The study's findings may provide new information that may help to fill the existing knowledge gap about the barriers immigrants are faced with in advancing to leadership positions. This study may contribute to an impetus for bringing about change in some organizations to make it easy for qualified immigrants to advance to leadership positions (Rumano, 2009). By exploring the barriers immigrants in mid to senior leadership positions faced in attaining leadership positions, the study may provide useful information to immigrants that they may need in order to better understand the steps to take and the pitfalls to avoid preparing for advancing to top leadership positions (Wamwara-Mbugua, Cornwell, & Boller, 2006; Wamwara-Mbugua & Cornwell, 2010). The study may encourage immigrants to explore ways that will assist them to advance to leadership positions. It is hoped that the study may also serve as a resource for Kenyan immigrants living in other regions within the United States or other western countries who aspire to succeed in attaining leadership positions in their host countries.

The Significance of the Study to Leadership. As a result of this study, the field of leadership may benefit from increased knowledge of leadership challenges immigrants who aspire to be leaders in various fields face in the United States and enact strategies to overcome them (Rumano, 2009). This is important because immigrants play a significant role in the growth of the U.S. economy (Hart & Acs, 2011). The knowledge gained may help in understanding the need to nurture and embrace immigrants who are a valuable resource to the United States economy and preserve its legacy as a land of freedom and opportunity (Davies, 2009; Hart & Acs, 2011; Takougang & Tidjani, 2009; USCIS, 2015). The United States diversity contributes toward positioning the country as the leader in the global economy (Davies, 2009). Exploring the impact of barriers Kenyan immigrants in mid to senior leadership positions faced in advancing to leadership positions may also persuade organizational leaders to be more open and tolerant of diversity and understand that immigrants make positive contributions to the society and the U.S. economy (Davies, 2009).

Nature of Study

The approach that was adopted in this study was a qualitative research method and a phenomenological design. A qualitative phenomenological approach was adopted in exploring firsthand lived experiences and perceptions of Kenyan immigrants who held mid to senior level management positions in Northern California. Leedy and Ormrod (2010) indicated that the qualitative approach was appropriate for data collection when a researcher was exploring the nature of a situation, relationships, systems, settings, processes or people. The qualitative research study involved describing and clarifying human experience as it is perceived in people's lives (Daly, 2007; Gill, Stewart, Treasure, & Chadwick, 2008; Polkinghorne, 2005). Qualitative phenomenological research is the experience as it is undergone, as lived, as felt, as made sense of, and as accomplished by people (Leedy & Ormrod, 2010). Polkinghorne (2005) posited that qualitative research data is collected in a form of spoken words or written language. In a qualitative study, data collection occurs through conducting interviews with subjects, observation, documents, pictures, and arts (Christensen, Johnson, & Turner, 2010). While quantitative research study is used to measure the relationships among two or more variables (Christensen et al., 2010).

The problem statement and purpose of the study supported

the phenomenological research design, the collection of honest views from Kenyan immigrants in mid to senior management positions who experienced some barriers in attaining leadership positions in private and public organizations in Northern California. The phenomenological research method is "the study of the meaning of experiences from an individual's own subjective perspective" (Greenfield & Jensen, 2010, p. 1189). Gee, Loewenthal, and Cayne (2013) suggested that the focus of phenomenological design is to return to the world of experience as lived. Using a phenomenological research design was an attempt at gaining a deeper and better understanding of the meaning or nature of experiences of the phenomena (Cilesiz, 2011).

The phenomenological research design was used to explore what an experience meant for individuals or participants who had the experience (Moustakas, 1994). The individuals or participants provided a detailed account of experiences, and general or universal meanings were derived (Moustakas, 1994). The goal of using a phenomenological design was to collect views from actual individuals who experienced the phenomena (Groenewald, 2004). Experiences were derived from the source.

Teddlie and Yu (2007) indicated that the flexibility of the phenomenological design might leave room for personal influence and bias. To overcome or minimize personal influence and bias in the study, the bracketing technique was used to focus on the phenomena (Gee, Loewenthal et al., 2013). Bracketing involved the researcher being aware of and putting on hold personal assumptions, judgments, and theories about the phenomena, while describing participants' experiences (Gee, Loewenthal et al., 2013; Mapp, 2008). The importance of using the phenomenological research design was the tendency of focusing only on participants (Gee, Loewenthal et al., 2013). The phenomenological research design was used to explore and find out what an experience meant for the participants who had the experience (Moustakas, 1994).

The goal of a phenomenological research design was to capture lived experiences of the subjects under study (Simon, 2006). The focus of phenomenological research study was subjective lived experiences of the individual and a description of the experience itself (Simon, 2006). Using a phenomenological design, the Kenyan immigrants in mid to senior management positions described the lived experiences and perspectives regarding barriers they faced in attaining leadership positions in private and public organizations in Northern California.

The qualitative research study uses an inductive approach that focuses on specific situations or people using words or description rather than using numbers (Maxwell, 2005). The qualitative method was the best approach for exploring the research question, which focused on understanding the barriers Kenyan immigrants in mid to senior management positions faced in attaining leadership positions. A quantitative research method was inappropriate for the study simply because the method is used to measure the relationship between two or more variables (Christensen et al., 2010). A quantitative method approach involves collecting numerical data using surveys or experiments while a qualitative method involves collecting data through conducting interviews and observing participants (Neuman, 2009). This study used face-to-face interviews to collect data, which is associated with a qualitative method.

The phenomenological design was suitable for this study rather than case study design. The phenomenological design was suitable because it was used to explore the perception of barriers Kenyan immigrants in mid to senior management positions faced in attaining leadership positions in various organizations in Northern California (Neuman, 2009). The case study could not work on perception. The case study also required extended periods of time to collect data and resources, which were not available (Neuman, 2009).

The sample for this study came from Kenyan immigrants' community residing in Northern California. The sample size constituted 20 purposefully selected Kenyan immigrants (Leedy & Ormrod, 2010). The chosen sample size was ideal because qualitative research is not concerned with the breadth of the research, but depth (Maxwell, 1998). The participants who were selected for the study were holding mid to senior level management positions in any industry or organization, were Kenyan-born immigrants, and residents of Northern California.

Face-to-face interviews, observations and audio recorded responses, were used to collect data from the Kenyan immigrant participants' experiences regarding barriers they faced in attaining leadership positions in private and public organizations in Northern California. Carefully worded interview questions were used to collect data from participants (Neuman, 2009). This study involved interacting with participants, observing, asking open-ended questions and interviewing until data saturation was achieved.

A research instrument was designed and used to collect interview data for the present phenomenological research study. The research instrument (see Appendix A) contained open-ended interview questions that were used to elicit the Kenyan immigrants' experiences and perceptions regarding barriers faced in attaining leadership positions in private and public organizations in Northern California. The designing of interview questions was guided by the research question and the objective of this study. The interview questions were used to provide an opportunity for participants to offer information freely and in detail on lived experiences and perceptions.

Two Kenyan immigrants, one holding mid-level, and another senior-level management position were selected to participate in a pilot test using the interview questions (Chenail, 2011). The data that was collected or information received from the pilot test was processed as usual, analyzed, and interpreted according to the objective of this study. The results of the pilot test were used to make adjustments or re-wording of interview questions if needed in preparation for data collection. The two participants selected to take part in the pilot test were excluded from participating in the actual or main study.

In this study, a systematic approach was used for collecting data and interpretive analysis of the data. The seven steps of Van Kaam's method of data analysis were used for analyzing digital recordings and transcribed interviews (Moustakas, 1994). Van Kaam's data analysis method was an acceptable methodology used in analyzing qualitative phenomenological data. The seven steps process began with a broad overview of data that was collected and it was filtered or narrowed down into useful or helpful information to identify themes. NVivo 11 qualitative research software was used for exploring, understanding, and identifying themes in this study (QSR International, 2016). The themes that emerged were recorded and evaluated for use in future studies.

The type of phenomenological research design that informed the study was empirical phenomenological research. The focus of empirical phenomenology was on self-reflection based on the phenomenon under study as well as participants' lived experiences with the phenomena (Hein & Austin, 2001). The empirical phenomenological research relied on the actual words that participants used to communicate the experiences (Hein & Austin, 2001). Considering interviews for this study were conducted using Kenyan immigrants, an empirical phenomenological design was appropriate and useful. In an empirical phenomenological research study, the design of the study has to be specific, the steps taken to obtain the results and findings formalized (Cope, 2005). The process makes the results and findings of the study verifiable so that the results may be used as evidence to understand the phenomenon under analysis. The process is completed by coding participants' responses into specific trends and themes (Moustakas, 1994; Simon, 2006).

Research Questions

Research questions are used to guide studies for the kinds of data that researchers will collect and suggest how the collected data will be analyzed and interpreted (Leedy & Ormrod, 2010). The first challenge in a phenomenological research study is to arrive at a topic and to formulate a research question that has a social meaning and personal significance. The research question must be clearly stated, key words defined, discussed and clarified so that the intent and purpose of the study is clear. The present qualitative phenomenological research study was used in exploring experiences and perceptions of Kenyan immigrants in mid to senior management positions in Northern California, to better understand what they perceived to be barriers to attaining leadership positions. The research question under consideration in this study was:

R1: How do Kenyan immigrants in mid to senior management positions perceive and describe their experiences on barriers in attaining leadership positions?

The research question was used to establish the scope or set the parameter of the research. In essence, the research questions are guidelines for the purpose of the study and help in exploring specific issues that the study will address.

Theoretical Framework

The theoretical framework was about the theories that were used to guide the study and involved incorporating theories relevant to the study (Rocco & Plakhotnik, 2009). The purpose of this qualitative phenomenological research study was to explore the lived experiences and perceptions of Kenyan immigrants in mid to senior management positions to better understand barriers impeding promotion opportunities to leadership positions in Northern California. The present study was informed by three theoretical viewpoints. First, the transformational leadership theory emphasized that trust was an essential element of effective leadership and created a climate that was supportive and receptive to new ideas from people (Jogulu & Wood, 2007; Wan Khairuzzaman, Hussain, & Muhammad, 2011). Second, there was the transactional leadership theory that involved the promise of rewards based on performance (Ali & Waqar, 2013; Jogulu & Wood, 2007). Third, there was the Leadership Practices Inventory (LPI) model which identified five exemplary leadership behaviors that produce success in any modern day organizations (Hutton, 2012; Sessoms, 2004). The results of this study may offer tentative recommendations as to the need to develop a defined organizational culture of trust in organizations as well as leadership styles for the Kenyan immigrants.

According to Lemay (2009), the traditional top-down view of leadership is still common in public institutions, yet modern public functions include additional public service stakeholders such as agencies, partners, and community organizations. Lemay (2009) argued that "the notions of results, efficient and effective management, and quality of services and ethics" are becoming the norm, and "there is a need to better understand the practice of leadership in the public sphere" (p. 3). The hierarchical form of leadership as practiced in the public sector, in relation to followers or subordinates may be explained by transformational and transactional concepts of leadership.

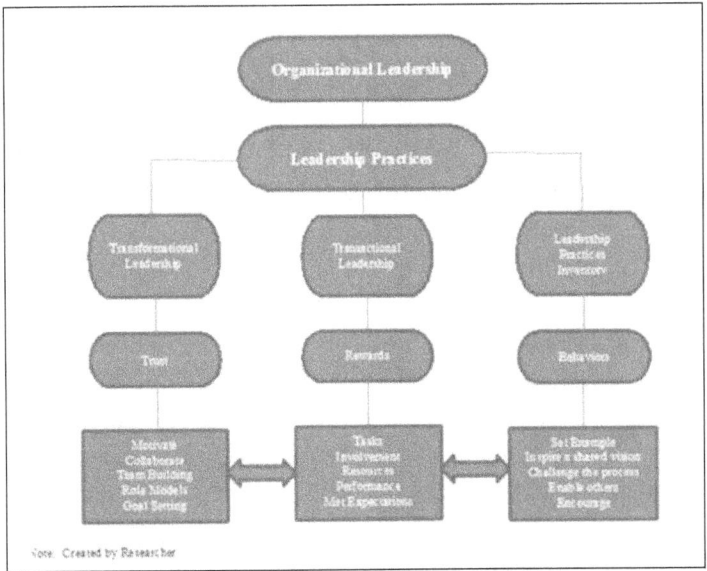

Figure 1: Summary of theoretical framework

Transformational Leadership Theory: Kouzes and Posner (2001) posited that transformational leadership is a form of leadership that builds trust in followers and trust is an essential element of effective leadership. A transformational leader creates an environment that fosters trust through the leader's ability to influence and to create a climate which is supportive and receptive to new ideas from followers or people (Jogulu & Wood, 2007). Transformative leadership demands upright behavior that requires self-transformation and the ability to reframe on how one views the world (Bolman & Deal, 2013; Caldwell, Dixon, Floyd, Chaudoin, Post, & Cheokas, 2012).

After gaining the trust and confidence from followers, a transformational leader is recognized as a role model (Jogulu & Wood, 2007). The purpose of this type of leadership is to develop, empower, and mentor employees to excel (Wan Khairuzzaman et al., 2011). These leaders are able to communicate effectively the vision to followers and create awareness of the organization's direction. These leaders also have the ability to support the creativity of followers, motivate, inspire, and nurture (Jogulu & Wood, 2007). Transformational leaders are concerned and actively involved in the work process and also take a personal interest in developing staff and in the success of individual staff members (Jogulu & Wood, 2007; Nielsen, 2013).

The transformational leader exhibits a high level of involvement and collaboration between leaders and subordinates (Jogulu & Wood, 2007). These leaders are change agents involved in creating the work environment and culture fostering change and growth (Nielsen, 2013). A transformative leader from the Kenyan immigrant community may play a central role because the theory demonstrates a commitment to the well-being of others and make leaders credible and trusted (Caldwell et al., 2012). Montuori (2010) indicated that a transformative leader combines soft and hard power, emotional intelligence, and analytical intelligence. The leader is soft on people and hard on organizational task (Montuori, 2010). This type of leader encourages, listens, leads, and follows and is decisive and reflective. Based on these characteristics, a Kenyan immigrant who adopted this leadership style would probably be successful in advancing toward attaining top leadership positions in any organization.

Transactional Leadership Theory: Transactional leadership style involves the promise of rewards or resources based on performance (Ali & Waqar, 2013; Jogulu & Wood, 2007). Leaders reward workers due to good work and withhold rewards when expectations are not met. Leaders exhibiting this style are actively involved in helping subordinates to perform and accomplish organizational goals (Abdul & Javed, 2012). The goals of transactional leaders are to ensure followers complete assigned tasks promptly and are rewarded for the effort and meeting expectations.

Leaders practicing transactional leadership style make followers aware of organizational tasks and rewards that are attached to those responsibilities. Leaders provide task clarity to staff, increasing the likelihood of efficiency, and believe in a give and take relationship by identifying followers' needs, and exchange rewards for acceptable results (Wan Khairuzzaman et al., 2011). This leadership style is effective where speed is required for quick decision-making and to maintain or increase organizational performance (Jogulu & Wood,

2007). This type of leadership could be appropriate for use by Kenyan immigrant managers when rewarding followers based on acceptable performance but may require using it along with transformational leadership style for effectiveness.

Leadership Practices Inventory Model: The LPI model enables individuals and organizations to assess personal leadership capabilities. Leaders, using the LPI model, may gain insight into how individuals see themselves as leaders, how others view them, and what actions can be taken to improve effectiveness (Kouzes & Posner, 2003). The LPI model involved studying five practices of exemplary leadership behaviors that produce success in any private or public organization (Hutton, 2012; Sessoms, 2004). A leader who exhibits the five exemplary leadership behaviors in any environment, including Kenyan immigrants, may succeed in transforming it. These leadership behaviors includes: (a) modeling the way, (b) inspiring a shared vision, (c) challenging the process, (d) enabling others to act, and (e) encouraging the heart (Boyd, 2014; Gentry, 2009; Hutton, 2012; Kahn, 2008; Kouzes & Posner, 2002).

Kouzes and Posner (2003) posited that leaders must always lead from the front, clarify values, and serve as an example for followers. An exemplary leader gains commitment and achieves the highest standards by modeling the behavior expected from others (Kouzes & Posner, 2012b). Inspiring a shared vision means that leaders would envision the future and ensures others buy into the vision (Kouzes & Posner, 2003). The leader's vision may not bear fruits unless followers understand and see what it is the team or organization is trying to accomplish.

Challenging the process involves leaders searching for opportunities, performing experiments and taking risks by constantly looking for or generating small wins and learning from their experiences (Kouzes, & Posner, 2012a). The leader is responsible for constantly looking for opportunities and taking initiatives in looking outside of the organization for innovative strategies to improve (Kouzes & Posner, 2007). Enabling others into acting involves leaders strengthening others and fostering collaboration (Kouzes & Posner, 2012a). Achieving a grand dream, Kouzes and Posner (2012b) wrote, requires a team effort, group collaboration, and individual accountability. Encouraging the heart involves leaders recognizing people's contributions and celebrates values and victories (Kouzes & Posner, 2012a). Kouzes and Posner (2012b) pointed out that it is important that a leader shows appreciation for people's contribution.

Definitions of Terms

The terms or phrases used in the present research study may have unique or multiple meanings. The definitions of terms or phrases are provided to establish an understanding of the concepts as applied in this research study. Leedy and Ormrod (2010) argued that the researcher should define each term as it is used in the project. It is important for readers to know what the researcher means when using particular terms or phrases to understand the research study and appraise it appropriately (Leedy & Ormrod, 2010). The terms and phrases that were selected and were relevant to this study include

Assimilation: The term was used in reference to immigrants or their decedents eventually adopting the American culture while retaining some aspects of their cultural heritage.

Over time, most of their cultural traditions such as language, food, clothes and many others were replaced with the American traditions (Connor & Koenig, 2013; Delorenzo, 2015; Steinberg, 2014).

Culture: The term was used in reference to behaviors of a group of people that differentiates them from another, or how groups of individuals or communities behave, or the values shared by those groups (Steers, Sanchez-Runde, & Nardon, 2010). Culture also include the knowledge, beliefs, morals, laws, customs or traditions, and any other attributes that were acquired by individual members of society (Burnard & Naiyapatana, 2004)

Foreign Born or Immigrants: The terms foreign born or immigrants were used in reference to individuals who were not U.S. citizens at birth. These include those who were naturalized U.S. citizens, legal permanent residents, temporary migrants such as international students, refugees, asylum seekers, and undocumented or individuals who were illegally in the United States (Borah, 2013; Grieco, et al., 2010; U.S. Census Bureau, 2015).

Home Country: This term was used in reference to the country of origin of immigrants living in another country (MPI, 2015)

Host Country: This term was used in reference to any country that welcomes foreign-born nationals or people from another country over a period of time, whether temporary or permanently (MPI, 2015).

Integration: The integration term referred to the process where new immigrants mutually adapted to one another with the communities they settle in the United States (Connor & Koenig, 2013; Jimenez, 2011).

Kenyan-born or Kenyan Immigrants: The term Kenyan-born or immigrants was used in reference to individuals who are of Kenyan national origin (MPI, 2015).

Leadership: The term leadership was used in reference to those who had the ability to motivate and influence the activities of a group or organization toward achieving shared objectives (Nielsen, 2013; Yukl, 2013). Leadership is the key factor in determining an organization's success (Bass, 2003).

Assumptions

Leedy and Ormrod (2010) contended that assumptions are the bedrock upon which the research must rest. The readers should know what the researcher assumes is true with respect to the study. This research study was based on several assumptions as follows. The first assumption was that participants who were selected to be interviewed would answer questions in an honest, truthful, and candid manner because they were volunteering and were assured that their identity would be kept confidential. The second assumption was that the experience of each participant was unique and special (Neuman, 2009). The third assumption was that participants' experiences were similar to experiences of other Kenyan immigrants in different regions in the United States. The fourth assumption was that the selected participants had the relevant knowledge that informed this study and would provide information that was relevant to the subject.

To ensure participants responded openly and without reservations, participants were given an assurance that their responses and identities would remain anonymous and confidential (Shuchman, 2014). Participants who were selected for this study were provided with a signed copy of confidentiality statement that indicated that this information would only be accessed by University of Phoenix's Institutional Review Board (See Appendix B). Each participant was also assigned a code to conceal personal identity (Shuchman, 2014). The use of codes encouraged the Kenyan immigrants to consent to take part in this study and share experiences during the interview. The personal connection of being a Kenyan Immigrant, the ability to speak the Swahili language, and residing in Northern California also encouraged the Kenyan immigrants to share honestly their experiences regarding the issue of barriers they faced in attaining leadership positions. Leedy and Ormrod (2010), suggested that face-to-face interviews have an added advantage because the researcher may be able to establish some rapport with participants and, as a result, gain their cooperation.

Scope

The purpose of this qualitative phenomenological research study was to explore the lived experiences and perceptions of Kenyan immigrants in mid to senior management positions to better understand barriers impeding promotion opportunities to leadership positions in Northern California. Simon (2006) posited that scope is important because it is used to establish the boundaries of the study. The scope of the current research study was limited to participants who were Kenyan-born immigrants currently occupying mid to senior level management positions in various organizations in Northern California. The selected participants had experienced the subject of the study and were members of the Kenyan immigrants' community.

Limitations

Christensen et al. (2010) indicated like any other research method, limitations exist in a qualitative research study. Neuman (2009) referred to limitations as threats to the internal validity that may reflect or reveal weaknesses in a given study. Limitations of this research study included obtaining interview responses from selected participants that were valid and represented the Kenyan immigrants' experiences and perceptions regarding the barriers they faced in attaining leadership positions in Northern California.

Because of time constraints, scheduling adequate time to meet each participant's needs and convenience was difficult, and this may have limited the number of potential participants. Participants may have also allocated inadequate time and availability for the interviews. Another potential limitation was that some participants might have chosen to give responses that were not honest or truthful based on personal experiences this study was looking for. Besides, some participants may have given short or long responses that made it difficult to decipher the lived experiences or beliefs. The sample size for the present study may have limited the number of willing participants for the study. Limitations of this study may arise from data interpretation, observations, or biased perspectives because of personal connection with the Kenyan community. Willis (2007) posited that the researcher should recognize personal biases and values and acknowledge them, and the researcher should make the reader of a study aware of those biases.

Delimitations

Leedy and Ormrod (2010) stated that "delimitations is what the researcher is not going to do" (p. 57). This study involved interviewing participants who were mainly Kenyan immigrants in Northern California. Participants that were se-

lected were restricted to only Kenyan-born immigrants occupying mid to senior level management positions in various organizations in Northern California. Each participant was
provided with an explanation of what the goals were for conducting the interview. Participants taking part in this study
were informed that the study was based on the need to understand the lived experiences and perceptions of the barriers
Kenyan immigrants in mid to senior management positions
faced in attaining leadership positions in Northern California.
Participants were informed that their identity was protected
through the use of assigned codes and not actual names to
maintain confidentiality and anonymity (Shuchman, 2014).
Participants were assured that information they provided
would only be accessed by University of Phoenix's Institutional Review Board and not any other third party.

To gain participants trust and confidence, codes were assigned for this study to conceal real identity and to facilitate
the free flow of information (Shuchman, 2014). Any information that potentially could be used to identify study participants were not disclosed (Wiles et al., 2008). Participants
were assured that signed informed consent form, demographic information, audio tapes, interview notes, and all confidential materials with individual participant's information,
will be securely stored in a bank safety deposit box and then
destroyed after three years.

To ensure responses were not biased, participants were interviewed alone at a private and secure location such as a reserved room in a library or a rented room at participants
convenience and to ensure they felt secure. Gill et al. (2008)
posited that interviews must be conducted in an environment
that is free from distractions and at times and locations con-

venient for participants. Participants were encouraged to take the time to provide detailed personal experiences and informed that responses to the interview would remain anonymous. In addition, participants were encouraged to be honest and truthful about personal experiences whether negative or positive.

Summary

In Chapter 1, a full review of the problem of barriers Kenyan immigrants faced in attaining leadership positions in Northern California was provided. Some of the barriers Kenyan immigrants faced while making an effort to achieve leadership positions included difficulty in adapting and integrating into the American culture, communication issues due to their accent, racial discrimination, marginalization, among others (Wamwara-Mbugua & Cornwell, 2010). The progress of Kenyan immigrants to attain leadership positions was hindered by the long process of assimilating to the American society.

One research question was also proposed in Chapter 1. The research question was used to explore the lived experiences and perceptions of barriers Kenyan immigrants in mid to senior management positions faced in attaining leadership positions. It is hoped that the answers to these research question and the results of this study may help Kenyan immigrants to better understand barriers impeding promotion opportunities to leadership positions.

Chapter 1 discussion included the background and the problem statement, the purpose of the current study, the significance of this study, nature of this study, and the research question. The chapter also included the theoretical framework relevant to this study, the definition of terms used in the study, assumptions, the scope of the study, limitations, delimitations of the study, and summary of the chapter. Chapter 2 involves the review of current literature, discussion of the historical overview of Kenya, historical overview of migration, Kenyan immigrants in the United States, cultural, social, political, and economic barriers experienced by Kenyan immigrants in the United States, leadership theories and models, and the literature gap.

Chapter 2
Review of the Literature

The literature searches for this study involved sources from 1963 through 2015. The early literature was used to provide a historical perspective on Kenya and history of migration.

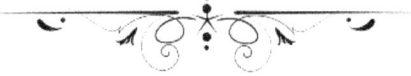

The purpose of this qualitative phenomenological research study was to explore the lived experiences and perceptions of Kenyan immigrants to better understand barriers impeding promotion opportunities to leadership positions in Northern California. The objective of the study was to address one research question: How do Kenyan immigrants in mid to senior management positions perceive and describe their experiences on barriers in attaining leadership positions? The goal in Chapter 2 was to review extant literature that pertained to barriers experienced by Kenyan immigrants in mid to senior level management positions in attaining leadership positions. Included in this chapter is an overview of the history of Kenya, a general overview of immigrants, Kenyan immigrants living in the United States, the cultural, social, political, and economic barriers to immigrants. Leadership theories and model and gaps in the literature were also discussed in this chapter.

Title, Searches, Articles, Research, Documents and Journals

Literature used for the current study was compiled using indexes and abstracts, online databases, online library, textbooks, government publications, articles, journals, various researches and the World Wide Web (Leedy & Ormrod, 2010). Most college and university libraries provided access to online databases with enormous collections of citations and abstracts related to various subjects and disciplines. The University of Phoenix provided EBSCOhost and Proust online library that was extensively instrumental in searching for relevant literature and articles applicable to the research problem.

The World Wide Web was a good resource for this study and included Google Scholar. Access to U.S. government publications such as the Census Bureau reports on immigrants, Department of Homeland Security reports, Department of State reports, Migration Policy Institute reports, American Community Survey reports, Citizenship and Immigration Services reports, and many other reports compiled over the years formed part of this study. The online search engines were helpful in retrieving the most recent articles and information about immigrants and Kenyan immigrants in particular. Articles with relevant information on immigrants and the barriers they faced in the United States were explored and pertinent information used in this study. Some of the literature searches were not relevant to this research study. The literature included a review of approximately 184 materials from various sources and, out of this, 69 were scholarly peer-reviewed studies. Table 1 provides a list of resources used.

Table 1.

List of the literature reviewed

Titles, Searches, Articles, Research, Documents, and Journals

Lists	Journals	Books	Peer Reviewed Articles	Other
Historical Overview of Kenya	11	3	9	2
Historical Overview of Immigrants in the U.S	9	2	8	7
Kenyan Immigrants in the U.S	11	0	4	9
Barriers to Immigrants in the U.S	27	6	16	8
Immigrants Career Development	4	1	3	1
Leadership theories and Leadership styles	13	9	8	13
Total	75	21	48	40

The literature searches for this study involved sources from 1963 through 2015. The early literature was used to provide a historical perspective on Kenya and history of migration. The literature review was also used to look at research in the area of barriers experienced by immigrants from other countries living in the United States. The leadership theories and model that includes transformational theory, transactional theory, and leadership practices inventory model practiced in private and public organizations were also examined. The aim of conducting literature review was to support the specific problem statement presented in Chapter 1.

The current study was conducted through a qualitative research method and a phenomenological research design. A qualitative phenomenological approach was adopted and used to explore experiences and perceptions of individual participants allowing them to give a description of their lived experiences in a natural environment (Moustakas, 1994). Qualitative phenomenological research is the experience as it is undergone or lived by people (Leedy & Ormrod, 2010). A phenomenological research design was used to explore what an experience meant for individuals who had the experience (Moustakas, 1994).

Historical Overview of Kenya

According to CIA Fact book (December 2015), the population of the Republic of Kenya was estimated at a little over 45 million people. The ethnic composition of Kenya's population included Kikuyu 22%, Libya 14%, Lou 13%, Kalinin 12%, Kama 11%, Meru 6%, Kisii 6%, other Africans 15%, and non-Africans, such as Asians, Europeans, and Arabs 1% (CIA Factbook, 2015). Kenya has 42 distinct tribes that have cultivated the history of the country (Yingling, 2013). The history of the Kenyan tribes is the history of Kenya, and, per Yingling's (2013) views, the tribal identities are also the cause of much division in the country.

Yingling (2013) posited that Kenya's tribal favoritism was the cause of the social, political, and economic problems more than corruption. The distinct ethnic languages, customs, and location are how to recognize the tribes of Kenya. In Kenya, people who lived in urban centers, as presented by the CIA Factbook (2015), constituted 22% while the remaining 78% lived in areas classified as rural or remote. This study focused on Kenyan-born immigrants who were living in the United States, and specifically, those who lived in Northern California regardless of their ethnic affiliation.

Kenya achieved her independence from the British colonial rulers in December 1963 (Hornsby, 2013; Hughes, 2011; Maxon, 2011; Wa Githinji & Holmquist, 2012). Immediately after attaining independence Jomo Kenyatta was named the first president of Kenya (Bannon, 2007; Kabukuru, 2013). Upon becoming president, Jomo Kenyatta advocated for unity, peace, and co-existence between Kenyans and the British masters. The reader should note that the British rulers colonized Kenya for 60 years before handing the leadership of the country back to the indigenous people (Hornsby, 2013). In fact, the country was colonized much longer than it has been independent.

When Kenya attained its independence in 1963, citizens enthusiastically celebrated the county's freedom from the British colonial rule with joy and anticipation of a bright future full of prosperity and social justice (Branch, 2011). The struggle for independence was behind, and people looked forward to a new Kenya. Hornsby (2013) explained that the Kenyan leadership inherited the country with the colonial ruler's structures intact and made no effort to make any changes. Some of the structures inherited were oppressive and were not suitable for the people of Kenya. Godwin (2002) contended that the social, political, and economic structures of the British rulers were retained in independent Kenya. The president made no attempt to overhaul the institutions and structures set by the colonial rulers (Kabukuru, 2013). Instead, the president used the same oppressive structures to promote ethnicity in its unequal development in governance and ethnic exclusion (Godwin, 2002). The issues of poverty, disease and ignorance, identified as enemies of the people in 1963 still persist (Branch, 2011).

Fifty years later, the people's dreams are yet to be realized because of challenges brought about by the political elite (Adar & Munyae, 2001). The country has experienced a more depressed economy than growth, increased ethnic tensions, increased poverty, increasing unemployment rates, expanding inequality, and injustice (Branch, 2011; Wa Githinji & Holmquist, 2012). The chaos witnessed in 2007 elections was a result of distrust, inequality, unresolved issues, and the poor turning to individual ethnic group to protect what the group had, and to attempt to gain more land or jobs to survive (Branch, 2011; Githongo, 2006; Mueller, 2009; Mueller, 2011; Steeves, 2006; Wrong, 2009). These issues and many others compelled most Kenyans who could migrate out of the country to improve their lives and that of their families. When Kenyans are presented with the opportunity to migrate, they do everything within their power to succeed. This explains their presence in many developed countries including the U.S.

Historical Overview of Immigrants in the U.S.

The United States of America was founded by immigrants

who came in search of opportunities and religious freedom (Jaggers, Gabbard, & Jaggers, 2014). It is fair to state that all Americans with the exception of native groups are either immigrant themselves or descendants of immigrants. The early immigrants in the first half of the 19th century came from Western and Northern Europe from countries such as Britain, Scotland, Ireland, Netherlands, German, Sweden, and Scandinavian countries (Delorenzo, 2015; Jaggers, Gabbard, & Jaggers, 2014). The early Africans who migrated to the United States came as slaves to work on the plantations until the end of slave trade in 1808 (Delorenzo, 2015; Rudolph, 2007).

The early immigrants migrated to the United States because of social, political, and economic reasons. Because of religious intolerance in their homeland, groups such as the Pilgrims and Quakers came to the U.S. in search of freedom (Delorenzo, 2015). Many governments in Europe were dominated by the land elite and, as a result, the common man had little to no say in the area of governance of their countries, and they chose to migrate to seek for freedom from oppressive regimes (Delorenzo, 2015). The early immigrants from European countries also came to the United States to seek for land considering land in Europe was controlled by nobles or the church (Delorenzo, 2015). The early African immigrants were brought to the United States for economic reasons that did not serve them but served the economic interests of the slave owners (Delorenzo, 2015). Overall, the early immigrants who came to the United States contributed to the building of the American Foundation through their ideas, skills, and culture they brought with them (Delorenzo, 2015). These immigrants formed the government, language, cultural traditions, constructed roads, and railways, brought farming techniques, and education traditions (Delorenzo, 2015).

The early immigrants as stated above were predominantly from Western and Northern Europe, who formed the government of the United States (Delorenzo, 2015; Jaggers, Gabbard, & Jaggers, 2014). This group of immigrants put in place various measures to regulate immigration. These measures included granting citizenship to selects groups and restricted who could enter in the United States and who could not (Jaggers, Gabbard, & Jaggers, 2014). The regulation measures included the passage of the Naturalization Act of 1790, the Chinese Exclusion Act of 1882, the Immigration Act of 1917, Emergency Quota Act of 1921, and Immigration and Nationality Act of 1965 (Jaggers, Gabbard, & Jaggers, 2014).

The Naturalization Act of 1790 for example, granted citizenship to white men who had a good moral character and who had lived in the U.S. for at least two years (Jaggers, Gabbard, & Jaggers, 2014). While women were only granted citizenship through their husbands or fathers (Smith, 2013). This act led to increased number of immigrants from Europe. The Chinese Exclusion Act of 1882 restricted the number of skilled and unskilled immigrant workers for up to 10 years, which could also be extended (Jaggers, Gabbard, & Jaggers, 2014). Any Chinese immigrant who wished to move to the U.S. had to demonstrate that they had exceptional skills which were difficult to prove. The act was designed to limit the number of Chinese immigrants coming to the United States.

Immigration Act of 1917 restricted illiterate immigrants who were over the age of 16 to gain entry into the U.S. and this was accomplished by administering of literacy tests (Jaggers, Gabbard, & Jaggers, 2014). To further slow down the flow of migration to the U.S., the Emergency Quota Act of 1921 introduced the quota system which indicated how many immigrants may gain entry from a given country (Jaggers, Gabbard, & Jaggers, 2014).

Immigration and Nationality Act of 1965 introduced changes to the immigration policy by providing each country with a limited number of visas per a year (Berlin, 2010; Briggs, 2012; Cadei, 2015; Casanova, 2007; Duleep, 2014; Jaggers, Gabbard, & Jaggers, 2014; Kandel, 2014). The act scrapped the rule of national origins and enshrined first-come, first-served principle that prioritized the recruitment of needed skills, unifying divided families, and on humanitarian grounds (Berlin, 2010; Cadei, 2015; Jaggers, Gabbard, & Jaggers, 2014; Kandel, 2014; Papa & Whelan, 2015; U.S. Department of State, 2015). Since 1965, Berlin (2010) posited, the number of immigrants entering in the U.S. legally increased significantly from approximately 3.3 million immigrants in the 1960s to 4.5 million in 1970s, and to 7.3 million immigrants in 1980s. The number of legally recognized immigrants in the U.S. towards the end of the 20th century tripled in size, and this number was higher adding illegal immigrants to the total (Berlin, 2010). In essence, the United States has been transformed into an immigrant society (Berlin, 2010; Cadei, 2015).

The Immigration and Nationality Act of 1965 also led to a surge of African immigrants to the U.S. (Kposowa, 2002; Kusow, 2014). Berlin (2010) argued that before 1965 black people of foreign birth residing in the U.S. were nearly invisible, and after 1965 there was a sharp increase of immigrants of African descent entering the United States. The beginning of the 21st century has seen more immigrants of African descent coming to live in the U.S. than any other time in the history of the country (Berlin, 2010, Briggs, 2012; Takougang & Tidjani, 2009). Likewise, the Immigration and Nationality Act has seen the number of Kenyan immigrants' increase rapidly for the last 40 years (Johnson, 2014; MPI, 2015; U.S. Department of State, 2016)

According to International Labor Organization (ILO), it is estimated that there are 232 million international migrants around the world today (ILO, 2016). The effect of globalization, shifts in demographics, political conflicts, income disparities, and climate change encouraged more workers and their immediate families to migrate in search of security and employment opportunities (ILO, 2016). Immigrant workers significantly contribute to the growth and development of their host countries, while their home countries become beneficiaries of their remittances, and the skills that are acquired during their migration experience (ILO, 2016). ILO (2016) indicated that the migration process is full of challenges regarding governance, protection of migrant workers, migration and development linkages, and international cooperation.

The International Labor Organization report estimated that there were 150.3 million migrant workers in the world (ILO, 2015). Migrant workers term was used in reference to all international migrants who were employed or were unemployed and looking for employment in their host country (ILO, 2015). The ILO's (2015) global estimates on migrant workers revealed that migrants form 3.9 percent of the total global population aged 15 years and above. The ILO (2015) report contended that migrant workers had a higher labor force participation rate compared to non-immigrants. Migrant workers constituted a higher proportion of 4.4 percent of all workers, which reflected a higher rate of labor force participation of migrants at 72.7 percent compared to non-migrants at 63.9 percent (ILO, 2015). This figure correlated with Kenyan immigrants in the United States, which showed that 93 percent of these immigrants in the U.S. labor force were employed (MPI, 2015).

Kenyan Immigrants in the United States

The movement of people has been around for a long time. People move from their home countries to search for a better life for themselves and their immediate families (Gilmore & Miller, 2013; Takougang & Tidjani, 2009; Yakushko, Backhaus, Watson, Ngaruiya, & Gonzalez, 2008). Immigrants leave their countries for various reasons such as the desire to improve their economic situation, unite with family members, to escape from wars, escape from civil conflicts, and environmental degradation (Hoyt, 2009; Kioko, 2010; Martin, 1999; Rumano, 2009; Ryan, 2008). Migration sometimes is forced and sometimes it is voluntary (Hoyt, 2009; McCabe, 2011; Ryan, 2008; Yakushko et al., 2008). The early Kenyans in the American soil, for example, were through slavery which was forced (Rudolph, 2007). The modern Kenyan immigrants migrate to the United States voluntarily in search of economic and educational opportunities (Gilmore & Miller, 2013; Odera, 2007; Wamwara-Mbugua & Cornwell, 2010).

The presence of Kenyans in the American soil has been recorded for over 300 years. The early Kenyans came to the United States not as immigrants but as slaves until it was abolished in 1808 (Rudolph, 2007). Voluntary migration of Kenyans to the U.S. began to increase rapidly after the Immigration and National Act of 1965 which removed migration restrictions and allocated each country with a limited number of visas each year (Berlin, 2010; Jaggers, Gabbard, & Jaggers, 2014; McCabe, 2011). Rudolph (2007) posited that voluntary migration for Kenyans to the United States remained negligible until the last decades of the twentieth century. For example, the number of Kenyan immigrants entering the United States more than double between 1980 and 1990 (Rudolph, 2007). The number of Kenyan immigrants to the U.S. continues to increase partly due to the close relationship between the two countries, availability of economic and educational opportunities, Kenya's depressed economy and high unemployment rate, and attraction to high technology oriented careers (Rudolph, 2007). The Diversity Visa program introduced in 1995 to citizens from countries that historically have low rates of immigrants to the United States has also led to increased presence of Kenyans in the country (MPI, 2015; U.S. Department of State, 2015).

Categories of Kenyan Immigrants

Kenyans migrate to the United States for various reasons and come in under different visa categories. The various categories of immigrants include visitors, students, Professional or skilled labor, and Legal Permanent Residents (LPRs). These categories of Kenyan immigrants were explained below.

Visitors: This category of immigrants are those who come to the United States as visitors with a nonimmigrant visa for a limited time (U.S. Department of Homeland Security, 2014). This group of immigrants includes those who come for business, tourism, vacation, medical treatment, seeing family and friends, or to attend weddings and graduations (USCIS, 2015; U.S. Department of State, 2015). Visitors are generally given visas to stay in the United States for 90 days or less (USCIS, 2015). But sometimes some of these visitors stay in the United States illegally or by changing or getting their status adjusted to either students or legal permanent residents (Odera, 2007).

Students: This category of immigrants are those who leave Kenya to pursue educational opportunities to build skills in the United States and hope to return to the country (MPI, 2015; Takougang & Tidjani, 2009). Kenyan parents value education for their children and do everything within their power to ensure the children succeed academically (Odera, 2007). Because of the high value placed on education, there is high demand for higher institutions of learning and Kenya does not have enough institutions to accommodate everybody (Odera, 2007). As a result, some parents strive to send their children abroad for undergraduate and graduate studies, and the United States is one of the favorable destinations.

Reports from the Institute of International Education (2015) indicated that the number of students from Sub-Sahara African region in the U.S. increased by 8 percent in 2014 and 2015 academic year to 33,593 students. Among these students, 3,072 came from Kenya alone (Institute of International Education, 2015). The reports also indicated that a large number of students from Kenya continue to attend U.S. universities compared to those from other countries in Africa (USCIS, 2015; U.S. Department of State, 2015). But due to global competition for highly skilled professionals and economic instability in their home countries sometimes students do not go back but gain permanent residence abroad (Kioko, 2010; Odera, 2007; Papa & Whelan, 2015; Takougang & Tidjani, 2009).

Professional or Skilled Labor: This category of immigrants are those who enter the United States as professionals or have special skills that are in demand (MPI, 2015; U.S. Department of Homeland Security, 2014). This group of immigrants includes professionals in the fields of healthcare, finance, technology and international business. Skilled labor immigrants come to the U.S. to work and hopefully go back home, but they too end up staying by having their status changed (Takougang & Tidjani, 2009).

Legal Permanent Residents (LPRs): This category of immigrants are those who come to the United States as Legal Permanent Residents (LPRs) or 'green card' beneficiaries (MPI, 2015; U.S. Department of Homeland Security, 2014). The migration policy institute revealed that in 2002 to 2012 fiscal years, the United States granted 72,000 lawful permanent resident status to Kenyan-born people, which accounted for 0.6 percent (MPI, 2015) of all those who were awarded green cards during that period. The Diversity Visa program is also another avenue used by Kenyan immigrants to gain lawful permanent resident in the United States. Introduced in 1995, the Diversity Visa program is open to people from countries that have a low population of immigrants in the United States (MPI, 2015; U.S. Department of State, 2015). Through the diversity program, 28 percent of Kenyan-born immigrants were granted LPR status in 2002 to 2012 fiscal years (MPI, 2015).

The Kenyan immigrants who are granted lawful permanent residents have certain rights and privileges that other immigrants from other categories do not have. These rights and privileges include owning property, living, and working anywhere in the United States (USCIS, 2015). Legal permanent residents are allowed to apply and become U.S. citizens after living in the country for five years or longer (USCIS, 2015; U.S. Department of Homeland Security, 2014).

Where do they Live?

Kenyan immigrants in the U.S. could be found in various states and preferred to live in large cities across the country. The majority of Kenyan immigrants lived in Texas, California, New York, New Jersey, Minnesota, Washington State, DC, Georgia, and Massachusetts (MPI, 2015; Takougang & Tidjani, 2009). Kenyans in the U.S. preferred living in large cities such as Houston and Dallas in Texas, Los Angeles in California, New York City in New York, Jersey City in New Jersey, Minneapolis-St. Paul in Minnesota, Seattle in Washington state, Washington DC, Atlanta in Georgia, and Boston in Massachusetts (MPI, 2015; Otiso, 2007). Kenyans preferred metropolitan areas because they tended to have many other Kenyan citizens, colleges and universities, and availability of job opportunities (Otiso, 2007; Takougang & Tidjani, 2009).

The state of California was one of the most favorable destinations with over 10,000 Kenyan immigrants (MPI, 2015). Kenyan immigrants preferred California due the large population of other immigrants, availability of many colleges and universities and many job opportunities (MPI, 2015, Otiso, 2007). The warm climate of California, which is similar to most parts of Kenya, was another contributing factor to the presence of large population of Kenyan immigrants (Otiso, 2007). The presence of many high-tech companies in California was another pull factor for Kenyan immigrants.

Barriers Immigrants Face in the United States

The purpose of this qualitative phenomenological research study was to explore the lived experiences and perceptions of Kenyan immigrants in mid to senior management positions to better understand barriers impeding promotion opportunities to leadership positions in Northern California. There was no doubt that all immigrants were faced with various challenges when moving into and working in the U.S. Some immigrants may have had more difficulties than others when joining the U.S. labor force. The common challenges faced by immigrants included difficulty in adapting or assimilating into the American culture, language or communication barrier, racial stratification, marginalization and education (Wamwara-Mbugua & Cornwell, 2010).

In this section, extant literature was used to explore the cultural barriers, social barriers, political barriers, and economic barriers immigrants encountered, and in particular, Kenyan immigrants faced in advancing to leadership positions in various organizations in Northern California. The literature review on cultural, social, political, and economic barriers was used as the framework for understanding what factors may have served as barriers preventing immigrants and by extension Kenyan immigrants from attaining leadership positions in various organizations.

Cultural Barriers

Culture: The term culture has many meanings in different

fields of study, groupings within society and what differentiates one society or organization from another. In this study culture was defined within the context of what differentiates one society from another. Culture, as defined by Dickson, Castano, Magomaeva, and Den Hartog (2012), are shared set of values such as norms, beliefs, and morals adapted by a particular group of people and defined the way of life for that group. While project Global Leadership and Organizational Behavior Effectiveness (GLOBE) research by House, Hanges, Ruiz-Quintanilla, Dorfman, Javidan, Dickson, et al. (1999) defined culture as, "shared motives, values, beliefs, identities, and interpretations or meanings of significant events that result from common experiences of members of collectivities and are transmitted across age generations" (p. 13). These two definitions and many others regarding culture have a common focus on shared values which are passed or transmitted across generations. This was an indication that first-generation immigrants moving from one society to another brought with them their cultural values to the new country for posterity (Gilmore & Miller, 2013). These immigrants were likely to experience culture shock and may have found it difficult to settle in their new society especially if the cultural environment was different from their own.

Culture and Leadership: The term leadership has a different meaning to different cultures. Dickson et al., (2012) explained that it is a difficult task to define the term leadership within a single or given cultural context, and it is even more challenging to explore differences in leadership across cultural boundaries. There is generally a common agreement among scholars that there are cultural variations in leadership, and there are aspects of leadership characteristics that are general or universal and those that depend on a specific culture (Dickson et al., 2012; Dorfman, Javidan, Hanges, Dastmalchian, & House, 2012; Lloyd, 2005). Universal leadership characteristics are perceived to be important across various cultures while cultural leadership characteristics are influenced by country-specific beliefs perceived as important and necessary to be successful (Bass, 1997). This makes the issue of immigrants complicated because migrating from one country to another with differing leadership characteristics make success difficult. In this regard, there is a positive correlation between culture and leadership characteristics because performance can be affected and may determine leadership effectiveness (Shah, Iqbal, Razaq, Yameen, Sabir, & Khan, 2011).

Dickson et al., (2012) contended that several authors have made an attempt to define leadership across cultures, and it had proven to be a daunting task. In an effort to define culture across cultures, the project GLOBE comprising of about 180 researchers conducted a study in 62 societies and after a long discussion agreed on the leadership definition as, "the ability of an individual to influence, motivate, and enable others to contribute toward the effectiveness and success of the organizations of which they are members" (House, Hanges, Javidan, & Dorfman, 2002). While Chemers (2002) attempted to define "leadership as a process of social influence in which one person is able to enlist the aid and support of others in the accomplishment of a common task" (p. 1). Dickson et al. (2012) combined the definition of House et al. (2002) and Chemers (2002) to define "leadership as an ability that is enacted differently across cultures, and as the process that is created and developed differently across cultures" (p.

486).

Dorfman et al. (2012) in their project GLOBE demonstrated that leadership behaviors are indirectly influenced by national culture. The research indicated that executives have a tendency to lead in accordance with leadership styles prevalent or endorsed by their particular culture (Popa, 2013). As a result, leaders whose behaviors meet or exceed society's expectations are the most effective (Dorfman et al., 2012). Dorfman et al. (2012) posited that it is important to understand the national culture as to which kinds of leadership will likely be most effective. For immigrants or Kenyan immigrants for that matter to be successful in the U.S., it is contingent upon them to understand and adopt leadership behaviors that are acceptable within the American culture. The failure to adopt acceptable leadership behaviors in the U.S. may explain the lack of advancement to leadership positions in various organizations.

Culture does have an impact on leadership considering different cultures view leaders differently. Individualistic societies such as the United States perceive leadership differently from collective societies such as Japan (Dickson et al., 2012; Lloyd, 2005). In individualistic societies, the success or failure of the organization is attributed directly to a single leader, while in collective societies, top leaders are not seen as the only source of the organization's success, but are held accountable for its failures (Dickson et al., 2012; Lloyd, 2005). The opposite is true to a country such as Kenya because the success of the organization is attributed to an individual but the failures of the organization lie elsewhere. Lloyd (2005) argued that hierarchical and egalitarian societies both have merits and demerits. The ideal culture may have both hierarchical and egalitarian approach and leveraging both approaches may be effective.

Dickson et al. (2012) contended that there are certain aspects of leadership that may appear to be universal across cultures and others that are specific to certain cultures. Bass (1997) argued that transformational leadership appears to be preferred, and it is the most effective across cultures. Transformational leadership can be participative or autocratic depending on how leaders in different cultures apply it to be effective (Dickson et al., 2012). In general, culture does have an effect on leadership across cultures. As in the words of Dickson et al. (2012);

> Culture does matter, and not in a small way. It matters in how leaders emerge, are selected, developed, and seen (or not seen) as role models to be emulated, and it matters in ways that are predictable, and that organizations can respond to strategically. (p. 491)

The study by Hofstede provided another dimension of culture and leadership which suggested that there are five dimensions of national culture describing routines, norms and attitudes of people (Moskowitz, 2009; The Hofstede Centre, 2015). The dimensions indicated that different countries have different ways of coping with inequality, relationship of the individual with his or her group, ways of coping with uncertainty, emotional implications of being born a boy or girl, and different ways of dealing with or handling the present and the future. The five cultural dimensions included power distance, uncertainty avoidance, individualism, masculinity, and long term orientation (Moskowitz, 2009; Shah et al., 2011; The Hofstede Centre, 2015). The five dimensions of culture are not the same all over the world, and affect leadership effectiveness in different regions differently (Shah et al., 2011). These five dimensions are explained below.

1. ***Power Distance:*** This dimension deals with social inequality and expresses the attitude of the culture towards these inequalities. This dimension indicates that everyone is unique, and that implies that all are unequal. People in societies exhibiting a large degree of power distance accept a hierarchical order in which everybody has a place. Power is centralized, subordinates expect to be told what to do, and the ideal boss is an autocrat.

2. ***Individualism:*** This dimension deals with the relationship that exists between the individual and the group. The dimension addresses the degree of interdependence a society maintains among its members. In individualistic societies, people are expected only to look after themselves and their immediate families. In collectivist societies, people belong to in-group that is supposed to take care of them in exchange for unquestioning loyalty.

3. ***Masculinity:*** This dimension expresses the dominant values in a society. A high score represents masculinity while the low score represents femininity. The masculinity dimension indicates a preference in the society for competition, achievements, heroism, assertiveness, and accumulating material rewards for success. The society as a whole is more competitive. The femininity dimension indicates a preference for being cooperative, modest, caring for others and the quality of life. The society as a whole is more consensus-oriented.

4. ***Uncertainty Avoidance:*** This dimension focuses on the extent members of a culture feel threatened by ambiguous or unknown situations and have learned different

ways to deal with these. Countries that exhibit strong uncertainty avoidance tend to maintain rigid codes of beliefs and behaviors, while societies with weak uncertainty avoidance tend to maintain a more relaxed attitude in which practice counts more than principles.

5. ***Long Term Orientation:*** This dimension expresses how each society maintains some links with its past while dealing with the present and future challenges. Each society prioritizes the two existential goals differently. A society with a culture that scores low on long term orientation dimension indicates that the society's preference is to maintain their traditions and norms and is suspicious of change. A society with a high score culture indicates that it encourages thrift and efforts in modern day education as a way to prepare for the future (Minkov & Hofstede, 2011; The Hofstede Centre, 2015).

Cross Cultural Communication: Giri (2006) argued that culture and communication are directly connected and have a great influence on each other. The culture in which an individual was brought up influences how they communicate and how they communicate can change the culture (Giri, 2006). Leonard, Scotter and Pakdil (2009) posited that culture influences what people communicate, to whom, and how they communicate. Cultural differences can sometimes make communication process complicated because of the variations in interpersonal interactions (Leonard et al., 2009). The success or failure of business ventures, for example, can be linked to the quality of communication. The communication style of Kenyan immigrants may be different from that of the Americans and may play a role in leadership determination process.

Besides communication which is influenced by how individuals from different cultures interact, communication is also linked to leadership abilities. Tourish and Jackson (2008) argued that leadership is a process that depends on the influence between leaders and their followers, and communication is at the heart of leadership. Leaders must possess the ability to communicate effectively with followers and stakeholders. Communication and leadership is important because it can determine the organization's success or failure in achieving its goals (Tourish & Jackson, 2008). Leaders must have the ability to communicate effectively the vision, direction, and the future of the organization to followers and stakeholders.

Social Barriers

The motivation for most immigrants to move into the United States is the American dream that views U.S. as the land of opportunity whereby success is attributed to hard work and perseverance (Delorence, 2015; Takougang & Tidjani, 2009). Other immigrants came to the U.S. to seek for economic and educational opportunities (Ande, 2009; Annan, 2007; Kioko, 2010); others were recruited to fill jobs such as engineering, and medicine which require specialized skills (Kioko, 2010; Odera, 2007; MPI, 2015; Ryan, 2008). While other immigrants came to the U.S. to seek for religious or political asylum from intolerable governments in their home countries (Kioko, 2010; MPI, 2015; Ryan, 2008).

The literature revealed that there were many social barriers that new immigrants to the U.S. are faced with. Hurtado-demendoza, Gonzales, Serrano, & Kaltman (2014) contended that people are social beings and require social networks that provide social support, influence, engagement, and interpersonal contact for their wellbeing. Lack of social support may lead to social isolation which may impact the health of immigrants negatively (Gilmore & Miller, 2013; Shinnar, 2007). Borah (2013) concurred that lack of adequate social centers such as having a community center to go for information and recreation might add to the social isolation. Borah (2013) argued that some of the challenges of living in a hostile society include exclusion, loss of social roles in the host country, and lack of a support system. These challenges have a negative effect on cultural adaptation, sometimes resulting in depression and suicide. Some other social challenges immigrants are faced with include acculturation stress, religious exclusion, stereotypes, discrimination, and language barriers (Borah, 2013; Takougang & Tidjani, 2009).

Acculturation Stress: Borah (2013) also argued that from a multicultural perspective, all immigrants experience acculturation stress. Many immigrants lack social and emotional support from extended family members as they often leave behind important relationships in their countries of origin (Berry, 2003; Hurtado-de-mendoza, et al., 2014; Kameny, DeRosier, Taylor, McMillen, Knowles, & Pifer, 2014; Shinnar, 2007). Immigrants' sense of loss is also heightened by work-related stress and having to adapt to the new environment making the assimilation process difficult (Borah, 2013). The Kenyan immigrants, in particular, may have difficulty in making adjustments to the new environment in the U.S. and the adaptation process is often very slow (Gilmore & Miller, 2013; Wamwara-Mbugua & Cornwell, 2010). In essence, their work performance may be affected negatively.

Religious Exclusion: Religion is an important value to the life of immigrants (Gilmore & Miller, 2013; Foner & Alba, 2008; Wamwara-Mbugua, Cornwell, & Boller, 2006). Connor and Koenig (2013) posited that religion is an important value in the integration process of immigrants in western societies. Religion plays a role in facilitating or hindering the integration of immigrants to the society (Foner & Alba, 2008). Being actively involved in nationally dominant religious groups may provide immigrants some access to resources, and may also facilitate integration to the American Society (Connor & Koenig, 2013; Foner & Alba, 2008). Belonging to a minority religion, Connor and Koenig (2013) argued, may block immigrants' structural integration. The literature revealed that immigrants belonged to minority religions and, as a result, were subjected to exclusion that may include occupational mobility and access to tangible resources (Connor & Koenig, 2013).

Religion may also play a role in immigrants' to be subjected to public stereotypes and discrimination. Discrimination behavior toward immigrants may be prompted by visible signs such as headscarves or kirpas, religious habits, or one's religious affiliation based on names (Connor & Koenig, 2013). For example, the study by Adida, Laitin, and Valfort (2010) documented that French employers responded less favorably to Muslim than Christian job applicants. In essence, religion may play a role in excluding immigrants not only from securing employment but also from upward mobility.

Stereotypes: Many immigrants are faced with anti-immigrant sentiments as well as fear of employers and community members who constantly ask about immigration status (Borah, 2013; Connor & Koenig, 2013; Martin, 1999; Takougang & Tidjani, 2009). Gordon (1998) argued that some stereotypes are directed to African immigrants such as there are fears that African immigrants are too many in the U.S., they do not assimilate easily because of their race and culture, and take jobs that belong to the American people. Immigrants are partly to blame for recessions and organizations restructuring that have led to the loss of jobs and stagnant incomes for most families (Borah, 2013; Connor & Koenig, 2013; Gordon, 1998; Hoyt, 2009; Moody, 2006). The new immigrants also threaten the cultural integrity of the U.S. society because they don't speak English very well, they don't join the melting pot, and are too different (Borah, 2013; Takougang & Tidjani, 2009). These stereotypes may negatively affect the Kenyan immigrants to be considered for promotions to leadership positions.

Discrimination: Many immigrants arriving in the United States, particularly from the African continent, still find discrimination and prejudice prevalent in the American society (Delorenzo, 2015; Lucas, Rudolph, Zhdanova, Barkho, & Weidner, 2014; Martin,1999; Takougang & Tidjani, 2009). Wamwara-Mbugua and Cornwell (2010) posited that immigrants come to the United States unaware of racial classifications, and they are consequently forced to be assimilated as members of different racial groups. For example, immigrants from Europe are assimilated into whites, and African immigrants are assimilated into blacks or African Americans (Wamwara-Mbugua, Cornwell, & Boller, 2006). Racial stratification shapes the lives of all black people in the United States and that includes the Kenyan immigrants (Wamwara-Mbugua, Cornwell, & Boller, 2006).

Language Barriers: Immigrants coming to the U.S. are faced with the language barrier but not for the majority of

Kenyan immigrants. The majority of Kenyan immigrants speak and understand the English language considering the country was under the British colonial rule, but the accent becomes an impediment because it communicates that the immigrant is uninformed and unintelligent (McCabe, 2011; Wamwara-Mbugua, Cornwell, & Boller, 2006; Wamwara-Mbugua & Cornwell, 2010). The experience of first generation Kenyan immigrants as far as the accent is concerned may be frustrating and may play a role in impeding their efforts in achieving leadership positions (Ande, 2009; Annan, 2007; Wamwara-Mbugua, Cornwell, & Boller, 2006). Even after achieving academic success and many years of living in the U.S., it is frustrating to be considered unintelligent based on the accent (Ande, 2009; Wamwara-Mbugua, Cornwell, & Boller, 2006).

Political Barriers

Lack of comprehensive federal policy on immigration reforms was one of the political barriers that immigrants faced (Hart & Acs, 2011). Jaggers, Gabbard, and Jaggers (2014) argued that uncertain future exists in the United States regarding immigrants due to the devolution of immigration policy. The United States federal government has done very little to provide a comprehensive immigration reform policy and as such, individual states have taken it upon themselves to introduce immigration controls which are both positive and negative (Briggs, 2012; Davies, 2009). Examples are the states of Arizona and Alabama which use state powers as a tool of oppression rather than to legitimately control immigration (Campbell, 2011). Arizona and Alabama restrict service provision and providing employment to illegal or undocumented immigrants, and penalize any businesses that hire these groups of people (Johnson, 2011). In Arizona, all immigrants may be required always to carry their documents because the police may stop and question anyone about their immigration status (Briggs, 2012). Jaggers et al. (2014) stated, "Legal and social conditions have made immigrants easy scapegoats for American social problems" (p. 11). Even though a state such as Arizona's efforts is to force undocumented immigrants out of the state, it may also have a negative effect on legal immigrants who may choose to leave the state to avoid being victimized because of the perceived racial profiling (Briggs, 2012).

The state of California has similar challenges as other states considering it is one of the states with the highest number of immigrants (Hirschfield, Ross, & Silard, 2013; MPI, 2015), but it has chosen to take a different approach in regard to immigrants. The state of California takes advantage of the diversity of talents and skills which are abundant among the state's immigrant population (Hirschfield et al., 2013; Jaggers et al., 2014). There are a large number of low and high skilled immigrants in California and specifically in Northern California, which is the home of Silicon Valley, and this makes the job market highly competitive in every sector. The competition for leadership positions is high and may have partly played a role in lowering the chances of having Kenyan immigrants becoming leaders in their organizations.

To improve the unemployment situation for U.S. citizens, there are calls to shift the focus away from the extended family and toward nuclear family, and from unskilled to high-skilled immigrants (Briggs, 2012; Duleep, 2014; Hart & Acs, 2011).). There are increased calls advocating for tightening immigration law to restrict the inflow of families and spouses allowed into the U.S. to join family members already immigrating (Briggs, 2012; Delorenzo, 2015; Duleep, 2014). These calls also include eliminating admission of unskilled workers and only allow skilled workers to immigrate (Barone, 2013; Briggs, 2012; Hart & Acs, 2011; Peri, 2012). To be eliminated will also be the diversity visa program that allows immigrants from countries with a low rate of immigrants in the U.S (Briggs, 2012; Cadei, 2015). The efforts to change the existing immigration laws to cap immigration, to reduce or eliminate certain categories of immigrants to the U.S., communicate anti-immigrants sentiments (Davies, 2009). The general sentiments of Kenyan immigrants and other immigrants may be a feeling of being unwanted in the country and could affect their job performance and might play a role in leadership determination process (Kposowa, 2002).

Occupational Exclusions: In the United States there are occupations that do not allow the hiring of immigrants even if they are legally in the country. Legal immigrants may not qualify for certain occupations because they are not American citizens (Plascencia, Freeman, & Setzler, 2003; Tyler & Petsod, 2003). These occupations are especially in the federal government or organizations that work for the federal government. These jobs are termed as sensitive or because of security concerns immigrants do not qualify considering their loyalty may be questionable. The occupational exclusion further limits the Kenyan immigrants on the number of jobs available they can occupy and experience upward mobility.

Economic Barriers

Economic opportunity is the number one reason for immigrants migrating to the U.S. (Ande, 2009; Annan, 2007; Delorenzo, 2015; Gilmore & Miller, 2013). With high unemployment in home countries and limited opportunities, the U.S. is attractive and draws immigrants to seek for these opportunities (Annan, 2007; Gilmore & Miller, 2013; Takougang & Tidjani, 2009). Many immigrants came to the U.S. with high expectations such as envisioning roads paved with gold (Annan, 2007; Connor & Koenig, 2013; Delorenzo, 2015; Kioko, 2010). The majority of Kenyan immigrants coming to the U.S. are motivated by the desire to improve their livelihood in terms of economic and educational opportunities, which tend to be more promising (Gilmore & Miller, 2013; Odera, 2007; Takougang & Tidjani, 2009). Migrating to the United States requires a considerable amount of resources and often those who migrate are those with lower socioeconomic status, and as a result, the cost of migrating takes a toll on their finances, and they arrive with little or no funds and are economically disadvantaged from the get-go (Briggs, 2012). These immigrants are further disadvantaged by lack of knowledge and social networks to help them secure high paying jobs (Shinnar, 2007). As a result, Kenyan immigrants may struggle and have difficulty settling in the U.S because of economic and financial challenges, lack of access to quality education, and lack of social networks (Briggs, 2012). The challenges the Kenyan immigrants faced may play a role in their lack of growth in various organizations.

Financial Challenges: When most immigrants first arrive in the U.S., they tend to take low paying jobs that require minimum language skills such as restaurants, hotels, landscaping, janitorial, manufacturing, and many others (Shinnar, 2007). The skilled, educated and talented immigrants also have difficulty in finding jobs because their education and skills may not be recognized in the U.S. (Borah, 2013; Shinnar, 2007; Tyler & Petsod, 2003). As a result, they are forced to take low-paying jobs and these leads to low opportunities for job mobility as they may be passed over for promotion (Borah, 2013; Tyler & Petsod, 2003). Kenyan immigrants may be faced with this situation where their education in Kenya was not recognized by some U.S. organizations or institutions, and this is a loss of valuable qualifications. Individuals may be forced to take low wage jobs to enable them to go back to school to acquire the necessary education and skills to secure employment in their fields of study and work their way up. This indicates that immigrants and by extension Kenyan immigrants may take some time to be ready and position themselves to advance into leadership positions in their organizations.

Educational Challenges: Connor and Koenig (2013) posited that immigrant educational achievement may determine their economic success because it provides competences and valued credentials in the labor market. The level of education of immigrants regardless of their origin is a predictor of occupational attainment (Connor & Koenig, 2013). Due to the rapid technological changes and advancement (De Kluyver & Pearce, 2012), immigrants may be lacking required skills to attain leadership positions. The high cost of education may also prevent many immigrants from going to college. Immigrants lack financial assistance that may enable them to pursue higher education or acquire skills needed to grow in their organizations (Borah, 2013). Immigrants may not qualify to have access to scholarships, grants or loans to pursue the education that will enable them advance in their careers (Borah, 2013; Tyler & Petsod, 2003). Lack of resources or lack of financial stability may prevent Kenyan immigrants from acquiring relevant skills required to attain leadership positions.

Lack of Access to Financial Institutions: Immigrants when they arrive in the U.S lack financial resources, do not understand how credit works in the U.S. and have difficulty in obtaining credit needed to purchase homes, cars, or consumer goods or to start a small business (Borah, 2013). Lack of credit history denies immigrants the opportunity to start any business to manage and become leaders. It takes time to establish a credit history and immigrants have no choice but to take available jobs to take care of their families (Borah, 2013), and these not only affects their financial status, but also advancement to leadership positions.

Immigrants Career Development

Shinnar (2007) conducted a qualitative study examining career development among Mexican immigrants, and the findings indicated that career development for this group of immigrants was shaped by three variables that included individual-level, group-level, and contextual variables. The study examined barriers experienced by minorities and in particular, Hispanics that limited career development. Shinnar (2007) indicated that individual variables refer to personal characteristics and goals. While group variables refer to culture value orientation, the status of immigrants, and workforce discrimination. The contextual variables refer to the condition of the labor market and trends in immigration.

According to Shinnar (2007), barriers to occupational advancement at the individual level included language proficiency, education, work experience, and individual goals shape career progression. There is a positive correlation between improving language skills, experience with the labor market in the U.S., and career mobility. At the group level, Shinnar (2007) argued that being part of a group may shape career advancement. Cultural values may shape individuals assessing the desire for changing jobs or career progression (Shinnar, 2007). Workplace discrimination may play a role in career advancement for immigrants (Annan, 2007). Managers may be reluctant to promote immigrants because they are ready to take the worst jobs and also managers may not view them as promotion material (Bernhardt, 2003). Immigrant workers may also be confined to a segment of the job market with limited occupational mobility. On the contextual level, individual career paths may be shaped by the job market and trends in immigration (Shinnar, 2007). The characteristics of the labor market such as unemployment and economic slowdown may indicate the labor market is saturated. Immigrants may be reluctant to change jobs or accept occupational mobility because of job security. The perception that there are too many immigrants and increased competition for employment may shape the desire to change occupation or limit occupational mobility.

The study by Yakushko et al. (2008) posited that the number of immigrants and refugees to the U.S. continue to grow, and the reason is the search for adequate employment opportunities and career development. In the course of pursuing career development in the U.S., immigrants are faced with multiple obstacles such as career development after relocation, immigration stress, and individual factors in migration, acculturation, oppression and discrimination (Yakushko et al., 2008). After relocating to the U.S. most immigrants may face unemployment, underemployment or loss of professional credentials (Ande, 2009). Most immigrants are not likely to secure employment in their field of specialization, and they are forced to work at lower levels of their occupation (Ande, 2009; Shinnar, 2007; Yakushko et al., 2008). The difficulties immigrants experience in gaining meaningful employment may contribute to their mental health which may affect their career development in the U.S.

Migrating from one's country to another is a very stressful experience that can take a toll on individuals' mental health (Gilmore & Miller, 2013). Yakushko et al. (2008) posited that immigrants may experience stress related to acculturation process, feel lonely, develop low self-esteem, experience strain and fatigue, the perception of the inability to function in a new culture, social oppression, and many others. The ability of individual immigrants to cope with migration stress, and the ability to adapt to the new environment, may play a significant role in how they approach their career development goals (Yakushko et al., 2008).

The qualitative study of Kameny et al. (2014) investigated the career barriers that minorities in the behavioral sciences field are faced with. Kameny et al. (2014) posited that the U.S. has fallen short in the area of the diversity of its scientific workforce because diversity is important and it plays a critical role in the country's capacity for research development and innovation. Even though for several decades minorities in the behavioral sciences have been underrepresented, there has been little policy and training to increase their numbers. As a result, minorities continue to experience barriers in this field such as institutional barriers, cultural barriers, personal career and skills barriers.

Institutional barriers can crush the success of careers among underrepresented groups (Kameny et al., 2014). Kameny et al. (2014) argued that even though diversity is a declared value in learning institutions, informal practices and policies may still maintain power structures designed to exclude contributions of historically underrepresented oppressed groups such as minorities and women. Lack of institutional support and opportunities to career advancement may force minorities to be dissatisfied and frustrated or leave their professions further denying them an opportunity to advance in their careers.

The cultural barriers are related to insensitivity, misperceptions, and miscommunication regarding a researcher's gender or ethnic background (Kameny et al., 2014). The work of minorities may not be viewed as of quality, and they may be forced to work as twice as hard to gain legitimacy and respect from colleagues. The perception that minorities are hired because of the color of their skin and, as a result, less qualified may negatively affect their mental health. On personal and skills barrier, Kameny et al. (2014) posited that individual characteristics can be a challenge to career development. Family circumstances, personal character, social support availability, and ability to balance work and personal responsibilities, can pose challenges to one's career. Lack of skilled mentors and cultural conflict may also play a role in impeding career growth.

The literature review discussed so far has revealed that there are many barriers to career development for immigrants which also may be relevant to Kenyan immigrants. In this study, barriers to attaining leadership positions for immigrants were explored through the cultural, social, political, and economic framework. The next section was used to explore leadership theories and models that were applicable in this study. To be explored are early leadership theories and modern leadership theories and model.

Leadership Theories and Models

Yukl (2013) submitted that leadership theories are classified into four approaches that include the trait, behavior, power and influence, and situational. The trait approach was one of the early leadership theories that suggested some people were natural or born leaders who possessed certain traits or characteristics that others did not have (John & Moser, 1989; Yukl, 2013). The trait approach's emphasis was on attributes of leaders such as their personality, motives, values, skills, the level of energy, tolerance of stress, self-confidence, emotional stability, and integrity contribute to the effectiveness of leaders (Yukl, 2013). Empirical studies conducted in the 1930s and 1940s, however, revealed that traits alone could not guarantee leadership effectiveness (Nahavandi, 2012; Yukl, 2013). This led to the development of other leadership approaches related to behavior and effectiveness.

The behavior approach involved observing what effective leaders did on the job (Yukl, 2013). The behavior approach was introduced in the early 1950s after researchers were discouraged with the trait approach and began to observe what leaders did on the job (Yukl, 2013). The behavior approach was used to examine how leaders spent their time, and the patterns of their activities and responsibilities. The approach provided useful insights as to what effective leaders did on the job and how they did it.

The power and influence approach examined the level and type of power that was possessed by a leader and how it was exercised (Yukl, 2013). Power is important because it is used to influence subordinates, peers, superiors, and people outside the organization (Yukl, 2013). Power and influence shape the attitudes and behaviors of followers. The situational approach of leadership indicated that the prevailing situation determined the best leadership style (John & Moser, 1989). The situational variables examined followers' characteristics, nature of work performed by leaders, type of organization, and the nature of their environment. The situation influences the approach leaders to employ to achieve desired goals.

The following is a discussion of various leadership theories that were relevant to this study because studies have shown leaders have the ability to bring about change in organizations. Leaders may use one or more leadership theories for effectiveness. Yukl (2013) posited that it is common for leaders to use two or more leadership variables at the same time. Leaders do this to ensure the achievement of organizational goals (Yukl, 2013). Below is a review of some of the leadership styles that are relevant to private and public organizations.

Leadership Styles

Leadership is the key factor that determines the success of the organization (Bass, 2003). Bass (2003) argued that leaders are responsible for deciding what needs to be done and who make things happen in an organization. Leaders have the ability to motivate and influence the activities of a group or organization toward achieving its objectives (Nielsen, 2013). The leadership style is about an individual's way of giving direction, implementing organizational plans, and motivating people to make a contribution to the overall success of the organization (Malos, 2012). Members are motivated and encouraged to be part of the team or group and work together to achieve desired goals.

Chaudhry and Javed (2012) suggested that leadership style plays an important role in building a sustainable business or organization. An effective leader has the potential to improve the organization's productivity and gain a competitive advantage. Leaders have different and distinctive leadership styles that are closely associated with organizational performance and outputs. A style of leadership can become an asset to an organization and help in achieving desired goals. It is important that leaders exhibit styles that have greater potential to help the organization achieve its goals.

Explored in this section were different modern leadership styles relevant to this study or the most appropriate leadership styles Kenyan immigrants in mid to senior management positions could adopt in order to succeed in achieving and maintaining leadership opportunities. Chaudhry and Javed (2012) argued that, without an effective leadership style, it may not be possible for an organization to achieve its objectives. Leadership styles that are exhibited by leaders in organizations and discussed in this research study include transformational leadership, transaction leadership, and leadership practices inventory.

Transformational Leadership Style
Chen, Lee, and Barnes (2010) defined transformational

leadership as leadership that develops a sense of community in organizational members to be willing to attain the objectives of the organization. Nahavandi (2012) posited that the focus of transformational leadership is on establishing an emotional connection with followers and inspiring them toward implementing the organization's objectives (Nahavandi, 2012). Yukl (2013) suggested that transformational leaders appeal to the moral values of their followers or employees in an attempt to raise individual consciousness regarding ethical issues, and mobilize individual's energy and resources to reform institutions. Transformational leaders communicate the organizational vision and create awareness of the organization's goals. These leaders encourage followers to transcend their self-interest for the sake of the organization (Nahavandi, 2012; Yukl, 2013). Leaders applying this style work collaboratively with followers to achieve the objectives of the organization.

A transformational leader gets employees to perform and meet objectives using transformational leadership style's key indicators. Some of the key indicators, according to Kirkbride (2006) include recognizing what must be accomplished, provide resources required to complete assigned tasks, provide support, follow up to ensure the agreement is met, and provide recognition to followers meeting agreed-upon objectives. A transformational leader inspires people to the extent individuals are performing job duties without force or coercion (Ledarskapscentrum, 2009).

The transformational leadership style is a systematic approach that followers support and appreciate their leaders (Bass, 1985). Leaders exhibiting the style are capable of motivating followers to exceed individual potential in accom-

plishing collective goals (Raja & Palanichamy, 2011).
Brown, Birnstihl, and Wheeler (1996) posited that transformational leaders do more than setting up the simple exchange or agreements. These leaders motivate followers to do more than intended, planned or thought possible to move above self-interest and focus on the bigger goals of the team, group or organization (Arnold & Loughlin, 2013; Raes et al., 2013). This style of leadership enhances subordinates motivation, which may lead to increased productivity in the organization. These types of leaders believe in followers and are driven by a strong set of values such as loyalty, trust, and personal attention to followers, which leads to organizational commitment (Raja & Palanichamy, 2011)

Transformational leaders have charisma, inspire, motivate, and are considerate (Raja & Palanichamy, 2011). This style of leadership involves four distinct factors that include (a) idealized influence, (b) inspirational motivation, (c) intellectual stimulation, and (d) individualized consideration (Arnold & Loughlin, 2013; Brown et al., 1996; Hargis, 2011; Islam, Aamir, Ahmed, & Muhammad, 2012; Raes et al., 2013). Idealized influence involves demonstrating high levels of competence, effectively using power to enhance group performance, and making each individual feel uniquely valued (Islam et al., 2012). Inspirational motivation focuses on motivating and energizing followers, communicating the vision and expectations of the organization, pointing out possibilities not previously considered, and create a sense of mission and purpose (Arnold & Loughlin, 2011).

Intellectual stimulation focuses on stimulating creativity, encourage followers to develop skills required to think through and view problems and issues in a new way, and solving problems themselves (Raes et al., 2013). Individualized consideration focuses on leadership behaviors with an aim of understanding individual followers' needs and motivating them to develop their full potential in the pursuit of challenging goals (Hargis, 2011). Transformational leaders provide the organization's vision and mission, create a sense of purpose, and elicit the respect, the trust, and confidence from followers (Brown et al., 1996).

A transformational leader motivates followers through inspiration, setting challenges, and encouraging personal development (Pedraja-Rejas, Rodríguez-Ponce, Delgado-Almonte, & Rodríguez-Ponce, 2006). The transformational leader encourages followers to achieve collective standards through a sense of purpose, a common mission, and shared vision. This leader shares the organization's mission and vision with followers. Followers understand, accept, share the plans of the leader, and accept roles in the organization with enthusiasm. In this environment, Wren (1995) argued, the leader and followers' purpose become mutual, and the leader and followers create a support system for one another. Constant collaboration between the leader and followers is evident in this type of leadership.

Arnold and Loughlin (2013) contended that people, who work with a transformational leader, are motivated, highly engaged, committed to work, and more satisfied. It is a participative type of leadership but can be directive. The result of providing transformational leadership is a high level of performance and motivation (Islam et al., 2012). This is because the leader makes an effort to empower followers and to move beyond self-interest by providing ideal influence, motivation, intellectual stimulation, and personal consideration (Raes et al., 2013). In empowerment, leaders' responsibilities are shared with members of the team, and important decisions are made collaboratively and collectively (Yukl, 2006). This type of leadership, Wren (1995) argued, "shapes, alters, and elevates the motives and values and goals of followers" (p. 103). Transformational leaders set clear goals, communicate the vision, expect the team to do their best, encourages and supports the team, compliments and recognizes good work, focus on the team, and inspire staff. According to Clawson (2006), "Transformational leadership is seen as a process in which leaders and followers inspire one another to elevated moral conduct" (p. 390). In essence, transformational leaders motivate, develop trust, and achieve the greatest following.

A transformative leader can bring real change to any organization whether private or public (Eisler & Carter, 2010). Adopting this leadership style may be helpful to Kenyan immigrants in mid to senior management positions to ascend to leadership positions in their respective organizations. It is important to develop a relationship of partnership with followers. In a partnership relationship, leaders inspire, engage, and empower others (Eisler & Carter, 2010).

Transactional Leadership Style

Government institutions such as Kenya often have hierarchical organizational structures with authority exercised top-down, which is associated with transactional leadership style. Transactional leadership style is used to motivate followers by appealing to individual self-interest and exchanging benefits (Yukl, 2013). This type of leadership style involves leaders providing resources and motivates followers through promising rewards for accomplishing assigned tasks (Nahavandi, 2012). Followers are promised rewards when expectations are met and rewards withheld if the expectations are not met. The leader and follower are in an exchange relationship. The leader identifies what followers need and promises to fulfill those needs for meeting expectations or achieving acceptable results (Wan Khairuzzaman et al., 2011).

Transactional leadership theory is based on the premise or assumption that members agree to obey the leader when accepting a job or a role. According to Groves and LaRocca (2011), "transactional leaders influence followers by controlling their behaviors, rewarding agreed-upon behaviors, and eliminating performance problems by using corrective transactions between leader and followers" (p. 512). The leader expects total compliance and obedience and reserves the right to punish team members if agreed upon goals are not met. This leadership style rewards members based on performance effectiveness and satisfaction (Avolio & Yammarino, 2008).

The transactional leader prefers to reward behaviors that are aligned with stated performance expectations. In this style of leadership, the leader sets goals that are specific, measurable, attainable, and time bound (Ledarskapscentrum, 2009). The rewards that are expected are clearly specified. Kirkbride (2006) posited that a transactional leader sets clear goals, objectives, targets, and clarifies expected rewards upon successful completion of the task. The leader monitors progress toward achieving expected goals and provides assistance or feedback when needed. Once the expected goals are met, the reward is provided. The relationship that exists between the leader and followers is essentially based on the reward system. This is a situation where the follower meets the leader's expectations and receives a monetary or non-monetary reward for it (Kirkbride, 2006).

According to Bass (1985), a transactional leader identifies followers' needs and engages them in an exchange relationship that is based on the objectives that will need to be met. Hargis (2011) posited that these type of leaders reward followers for accomplishing agreed-upon objectives. The leader clearly sets the objectives and specifies expected rewards so that followers are aware of what will be received or voided if expectations are fulfilled or fail to meet expectations (Brown et al., 1996). Liu, Liu, and Zeng (2011) argued that, in a transactional leadership, leaders specify expectations, clarify responsibilities, negotiate contracts, and recognize and reward followers in order to achieve expected performance. In a transactional leadership style, followers comply, accept, and agree with the leader in exchange for praise, rewards, and resources, or to avoid disciplinary action (Liu et al., 2011)

Raja and Palanichamy (2011) posited that transactional leaders always set goals, articulate explicit agreements regarding what the leader expects from followers, defines how members will be rewarded for their efforts and commitment, and provides feedback in order to keep everyone on task. This type of leader provides followers something that is needed to receive something the leader wants (Raja & Palanichamy, 2011). To ensure the standards of performance agreed upon are met, the leader continually observes followers and initiates corrective measures when necessary (Hargis, 2011).

The focus of transactional leaders is to motivate followers through a system of providing rewards or punishments (Islam et al., 2012; Malos, 2012). These leaders provide materialistic or psychological rewards for efforts and recognize good performance. Malos (2012) posited that leaders intervene when subordinates are unable to achieve an acceptable level of performance and initiate corrective measures aimed at improving performance. The workload of a transactional leader is reduced because the leader is only called upon when workers deviate from established standards (Malos, 2012).

A transactional leader motivates followers through the provision of benefits, as long as followers are capable of completing assigned tasks (Pedraja-Rejas et al., 2006). The relationship could be referred to as mutual because it involves negotiations between leader and follower. In a transactional leadership style, followers understand and agree with the rewards system. Transactional leadership is suitable to solve short-term issues and cannot adequately address long-term contemporary leadership issues and challenges. The relationship between leaders and followers is short lived and sometimes nonexistent. Exchanging goods for money will not constitute a relationship but a transaction. This is unlike transformational leaders, who have a connection with followers until the task is completed or organizational goals are met.

The transformational and transactional leadership styles are both useful in contemporary organizations, and leaders can exhibit each style at one time or another in daily activities (Wan Khairuzzaman et al., 2011). A combination of both leadership styles may be effective and useful to Kenyan immigrants if applied appropriately in their respective organizations. Effective leaders can exhibit both leadership styles. Transactional leaders provide clear direction and are successful in time-driven tasks. The style is valuable, appropriate, and may lead to efficiency (Jogulu & Wood, 2007). Transformational leaders encourage active participation and collaboration between leaders and followers.

Leadership Practices Inventory Model

According to Kouzes and Posner (2002), the leadership practices inventory (LPI) model was developed with the aim of helping individuals and organizations to assess leadership capabilities. The leadership practices inventory is about the five exemplary leadership behaviors that produce success in any private or public organization (Kouzes & Posner, 2002). Leaders exhibiting these five exemplary leadership behaviors are in a position to increase individual abilities to lead others to accomplish organizational goals (Marshal, 2009). The leadership behaviors include (a) modeling the way, (b) inspiring a shared vision, (c) challenging the process, (d) enabling others to act, and (e) encouraging the heart (Boyd, 2014; Gentry, 2009; Hutton, 2012; Kahn, 2008; Kouzes & Posner, 2002; Marshall, 2009)

Modeling the Way: Kouzes and Posner (1992) argued that modeling the way involves translating shared values into actions, being accountable to one another, and influencing by example. This also includes breaking tasks into manageable steps to allow people to experience small wins while striving to achieve larger objectives (Kouzes & Posner, 2001; Yavuz, 2010). Yavuz (2010) posited that leaders are responsible for establishing principles regarding how people are treated and the way goals are pursued. Leaders also develop standards for others to follow and serve as an example. Kouzes and Posner (2012a) suggested that a credible leader must lead by example.

Leaders who model the way, Kouzes and Posner (2001) argued, put up signposts for people to follow when unsure which way to go or how to get there. Modeling the way is leading or influencing by example. Kouzes and Posner (2001) suggested that leadership is personal. It is a personal connection between the leader and followers, and the relationship is built on honesty. Leaders must be honest by telling the truth, and that includes admitting when mistakes are made. People will be more than willing to follow a leader who is honest, and can be trusted as a model that is worthy emulating.

The modeling the way attribute of exemplary leadership behavior is important and may be beneficial to Kenyan immigrants in mid to senior management positions to adopt. A leader who exhibits this behavior will succeed in influencing followers and stakeholders. Leaders set an example making it easier for subordinates to follow. Kouzes and Posner (2007) indicated that a leader must serve as an example to be successful. A leader needs followers as much as followers need leaders. Leaders and followers must work together to achieve shared objectives.

Inspiring a Shared Vision: Inspiring a shared vision involves the leader and followers having a common understanding of what the team or the organization is trying to accomplish (Kouzes and Posner, 1992). To have a common understanding of what the team or organization is trying to achieve, Marshall (2009) proposed that the leader must build a relationship with followers before expectations are established. People would work hard for something envisioned as important, and leaders may not know what people view as important until relationships are built. The leader must be passionate about the vision, share it with followers, and together imagine what the team or organization can become

(Yavuz, 2010). The leader and followers must be connected in terms of imagining an exciting and attractive future (Kouzes & Posner, 2012b).

This exemplary leadership behavior would be beneficial and appropriate for Kenyan immigrants in management positions to adopt. An inspiring leader must inform followers about the vision and the place of followers in that vision (Kouzes & Posner, 2012b). Followers need to understand the direction the leader intends to take, how to get there and the importance of achieving the vision. In essence, the Kenyan immigrants must stay connected with followers in order to achieve the shared vision.

Challenging the Process: Challenging the process involves willing to take risks, explore new alternatives, experiment, learn from mistakes, and support one another (Kouzes & Posner, 1992). Marshal (2009) posited that true leaders must be willing to experiment, take risks, and know that failure is always an option, or otherwise the process is never changed, and new successes may never be realized. This indicates that leaders must continuously search for new opportunities with the aim of making changes to the status quo and finding innovative ways to improve the organization (Yavuz, 2010). Kouzes and Posner (2001) wrote that leaders understand that taking risks involves mistakes and sometimes failures, and it is important to accept disappointments as learning opportunities. Good leaders, Marshall (2009) pointed out, must learn from mistakes and failures as much as success.

This exemplary leadership behavior is very important and can significantly improve the chances of Kenyan immigrants becoming leaders in their organizations. The Kenyan immigrants must continually search for opportunities within their organizations, must be willing to take chances, and if mistakes are made learn from them (Kouzes & Posner, 2001). This is because to transform an organization, leaders must take chances. A leader, who does not take risks, will maintain the status quo and never experience growth or success (Kouzes & Posner, 2001; Marshall, 2009). Organizations need leaders who are not afraid taking risks and are willing to experiment (Marshall, 2009).

Enabling Others to Act: Enabling others to act involves leaders setting goals and planning projects, sharing information, setting organizational objectives, keeping others informed, respecting other people's ideas, and being competent (Kouzes & Posner, 1992). Enabling others to act is also trusting and allowing others to take responsibility for tasks that can improve individual leadership skills. Leaders who allow employees to participate and fosters collaboration and friendship may inspire employees to do more. Leaders, who allow others to play a central role in the team or organization's decision-making process, are developing future leaders. To plan for the future of the organization, Marshal (2009) wrote, a true leader must build others up and be ready to take leadership roles in the future. Through delegation, the leader is indeed enabling others to act. Delegating to others builds trust and guarantees the continuity of the organization.

Enabling others to act leadership behavior is appropriate for Kenyan immigrants to adopt. It is important that leaders develop followers to take up leadership roles in the future. Leaders cannot remain in leadership positions forever. It is prudent for leaders to allow followers to get actively involved in the decision-making process. To plan for the future of an organization, the leader must develop others to take leadership roles in the future (Marshall, 2009).

Encouraging the Heart: Encouraging the heart means the leader is emotionally connected to the team or organization, providing feedback, acknowledging team or organizational accomplishments, and celebrating achievements and milestones (Kouzes & Posner, 1992). Marshall (2009) posited that encouraging the heart is recognizing people's contributions, celebrating victories, and rewarding hard work. Appreciating followers is a way of encouraging hard work and maintaining positive morale. Marshall (2009) argued that mini-celebrations conducted on a regular basis are necessary to encourage extraordinary accomplishments to happen. Encouraging people and recognizing individual contributions may prevent burnout and increase productivity.

Encouraging the heart is also beneficial and appropriate exemplary leadership behavior that Kenya immigrants in mid to senior management positions may adopt in their pursuit for advancing to leadership positions. This exemplary leadership behavior would encourage Kenyan immigrants in mid to senior management positions to recognize employees' collective and individual contribution toward the success of the organization. Everyone likes recognition and employees are no exceptions.

The transformational and transactional leadership styles are both useful in contemporary organizations, and leaders can exhibit each style at one time or another in daily activities (Wan Khairuzzaman et al., 2011). A combination of both leadership styles may be effective in private or public organizations. Effective leaders can exhibit both leadership styles. Transactional leaders provide clear direction and are successful in time-driven tasks. The style is valuable, appropriate, and may lead to efficiency (Jogulu & Wood, 2007). Transformational leaders encourage active participation and collaboration between leaders and followers. Jogulu and Wood (2007) suggested that a transformational leader motivates, inspires, and supports followers' creativity.

Gaps in the Literature of Barriers to Migration to Developed Countries

The purpose of this qualitative phenomenological research study was to explore the lived experiences and perceptions of Kenyan immigrants to better understand barriers impeding promotion opportunities to leadership positions in Northern California. Despite a wealth of existing literature regarding immigrants in the United States (Borah, 2013), there were very few studies that had been undertaken to deal with Kenyan immigrants in management positions in different regions especially in Northern California. The goal of this study was to examine the cultural, social, political and economic barriers that may have played a role in preventing Kenyan immigrants from advancing into leadership positions in their respective organizations. The literature reviewed did not contain actions that may be taken by immigrants to overcome these barriers.

The literature review included evidence of various challenges immigrants in the U.S. labor force faced, but scholars observed that different immigrants have different cultural, social, political and economic challenges (Berry, 2003; Cisneros, 2012; Portes, 1997; Shinnar, 2007; Wamwara-Mbugua & Cornwell, 2010; Yakushko, 2008). Shinnar (2007) noted that barriers to career development for minorities and in particular Hispanics included communication difficulties, lower education attainment, difficult finding mentors, coping with acculturation process into the U.S. society, the perception of workplace discrimination, the perception of limited opportunities for advancement, cultural value orientation and low socioeconomic status. Wamwara-Mbugua and Cornwell (2010) also indicated that the Kenyan immigrants, in particular, had difficulty in making adjustments to the new environment in the U.S., and the adaptation process was impacted by their race and colonial histories. It takes time to adapt and cope with the American culture and to shape the career progression of immigrants (Ande, 2009). Scholars in this literature review provided no clear solutions or steps to be taken to overcome barriers to career development for immigrants.

Few scholars had contributed to the literature about Kenyan immigrants' participation in the U.S. labor force, the barriers they encountered in advancing to leadership positions, and what may be done to overcome those barriers. There were hardly any studies that specifically addressed the cultural, social, political, and economical barriers faced by Kenyan immigrants. Scholars provided general observations regarding barriers encountered by new immigrants to the United States but provided no tangible solutions (Berry, 2003; Cisneros, 2012; Davies, 2009; Shinnar, 2007; Wamwara-Mbugua & Cornwell, 2010). The findings from the study may fill this knowledge gap which was important to Kenyan immigrants in mid to senior management roles and who wished to advance to leadership positions in their organizations.

Inadequate information on barriers immigrants in management positions faced in advancing to leadership positions contributed to underestimating its effect on the U.S. economy

(Hirschfield et al., 2013; Shinnar, 2007; Tyler & Petsod, 2003). The phenomenological study with the Kenyan immigrants in mid to senior management positions may provide some useful information to understand and create awareness of those barriers. The interviews from the study may lead to obtaining ideas from the Kenyan immigrants about ways to lessen the effect or overcome these barriers. The aim of the literature was to note the existence of barriers to immigrants' career advancement efforts, (Kameny, et al., 2014; Shinnar, 2007; Yakushko et al., 2008) and an existence of the knowledge gap this study attempted to fill.

Summary

Chapter 2 provided a detailed historical overview of Kenya since independence in 1963 from the British colonial rulers. The literature in this chapter included the history of immigrants and migration, Kenyan immigrants in the U.S., and immigrants' cultural, social, political, and economic barriers. The discussion in this chapter also included leadership theories and models that were relevant to this study, and gaps in the literature were highlighted and used in the final analysis.

The discussion in Chapter 3 provides a detailed explanation of the procedure and steps taken to obtain and analyze data for this study. The discussion covered areas of qualitative research method and phenomenological research design used to collect data, design appropriateness, and research questions that guided this study. The discussion also included population demographic, sampling, informed consent, issues of confidentiality, geographic location of the study, instrumentation, strategies for data collection, strategies for data analysis, reliability and validity, and a summary at the end of the chapter.

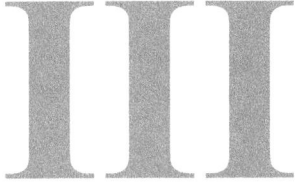

Chapter 3
Research Methods

Applying a phenomenology approach indicated the study was focusing on lived experiences of the people describing the phenomena as accurately as possible (Groenewald, 2004). The phenomenology approach focuses on facts or firsthand experience of the people involved.

The research method refers to the procedure or process that is used in making systematic observations to obtain data, obtain evidence, or information as part of a research study (Leedy, & Ormrod, 2010; Sharan, 1998). The purpose of this qualitative phenomenological research study was to explore the lived experiences and perceptions of Kenyan immigrants in mid to senior management positions to better understand barriers impeding promotion opportunities to leadership positions in Northern California. Information on lived experiences and perceptions of participants was obtained by conducting face-to-face interviews with 20 Kenyan immigrants who occupied mid to senior level management positions in their respective organizations. The finding from this study may contribute to an in-depth understanding of the challenges or barriers that Kenyan immigrants faced in attaining leadership positions in private and public organizations in Northern California (Neuman, 2009).

The Van Kaam's method that was modified by Moustakas (1994) was used for analysis in this research study. The method required recording and transcribing semi-structured interviews. The data collected from responses of the Kenyan immigrants' participants was analyzed using NVivo 11 qualitative research software (QSR International, 2016). The NVivo 11 qualitative research software was used to manage, sort, and arrange verbatim interview data for analysis (QSR International, 2016).

Chapter 3 provides a description and an explanation of methods used in collecting data, answering the research question, and providing information on Kenyan immigrants lived experiences and perceptions regarding the barriers they experienced in attaining leadership positions in their respective fields. A discussion and a detailed explanation of the procedure and steps taken to obtain and analyze data were provided. The discussion covered areas of research design, method and design appropriateness, research questions guiding this study, the target population, sampling procedures, informed consent, confidentiality, geographic location, and instrumentation. The discussion in this chapter also included data collection strategies, data analysis strategies that were applied, reliability and validity, and concludes with a summary.

Description of Research Design

The research design is the researcher's plan of action for answering research questions or a description of how the researcher will conduct the study (Knight, 2010; Sharan, 1998). The research design provides a description of how the research was conducted and how the data was obtained (Knight, 2010). Sharan (1998) posited that the research design is the planning and the organization of procedures or processes used to make observations and to obtain data, evidence, or information that will form part of a research study. The design for this study was chosen based on many factors including the purpose of the resulting data, type of respondents, social and economic attributes of respondents, time availability, and availability of financial resources for conducting the study (Neuman, 2009).

To address the purpose of this study, a qualitative research method was used along with a phenomenological research design. A qualitative research method is an approach used to explore and understand the meaning that individuals or groups of people attribute to a social or human problem or condition (Neuman, 2009). A qualitative study is about learning different experiences as perceived by individuals (Vishnevsky & Beanlands, 2004). The purpose of a qualitative research study is to explore what an experience means for individual participants who had the experience and were able to describe it in detail (Moustakas, 1994). A qualitative research process involves merging questions and procedures, data collection in participants' settings, inductively analyzing data, the building of general themes, and data interpretation (Leedy & Ormrod, 2010; Neuman, 2009). The research study involves the documenting of real life events, audio or video recording of what people say, observing behaviors of specific people, as well as studying written documents, or examining visual images (Neuman, 2009). Neuman, (2009) argued that qualitative studies are associated with conducting interviews, making observations, reading documents or transcripts, and critiquing pictures, recordings, and video tapes.

There are various types of qualitative study designs that include narrative research study, empirical phenomenological research study, ethnographic research study, grounded theory research study, hermeneutics study, and the case study (Moustakas, 1994). This qualitative study applied an empirical phenomenological research because it involves a description of participants' experiences with the phenomenon (Hein & Austin, 2001). Some of the features of an empirical phenomenological research study are such as its emphasis on the structure of the phenomenon of interest, the revealing of what the phenomenon is as lived human meaning, and its reliance on the actual words that are used by participants to communicate individual experiences (Hein & Austin, 2001). An empirical phenomenological research was appropriate for this study because it involved conducting interviews, recording the interview, and taking notes of responses from the Kenyan immigrants in Northern California to discover the phenomenon under study.

The phenomenological design was selected for the current study because of its inductive approach that is concerned with richness, texture and feeling for the raw data collected (Neuman, 2009). The research design was chosen because it is used to focus on lived experiences of the people (Groenewald, 2004). The phenomenological design helped to gain deeper and better understanding of the meaning or nature of experiences of the phenomena (Cilesiz, 2011). A phenomenological design and Van Kaam's seven steps method of analysis that was developed by Hursell and modified by Moustakas was used in this qualitative study (Moustakas, 1994). The Van Kaam's approach is an acceptable method used for analyzing qualitative phenomenological data (Moustakas, 1994). The method provides a step by step or systematic process researchers may use to analyze participants' transcribed interview (Moustakas, 1994). The Van Kaam's seven steps process start with a broad view of the data that is collected, and then filters it systematically into information that is useful to draw major themes from.

Method and Design Appropriateness

The qualitative research method was deemed as an ideal approach to this study because it is used by researchers to obtain accounts of life experiences of individuals (Vishnevsky & Beanlands, 2004). A qualitative research study involves a description and clarification of human experiences as it appears in people's lives (Daly, 2007; Polkinghorne, 2005). The qualitative research is an account of how people make sense of individual lived experiences (Daly, 2007; Ochieng, 2009). The qualitative research data is collected in a form of spoken or written language (Polkinghorne, 2005). In a qualitative study, data is collected through conducting interviews with participants, through observations, documentation, pictures, and artifacts (Bernard, 2013; Neuman, 2009). Qualitative research approach was useful in exploring firsthand lived experiences of the Kenyan immigrants in mid to senior management positions regarding barriers they were confronted with in attaining leadership positions in their respective organizations in Northern California. The qualitative research approach is suitable for exploring human experiences.

The quantitative research method was considered but found not appropriate or suitable for the study simply because the problem statement and the purpose of the study were aligned with the qualitative method. Quantitative research method requires the collection of numerical data through surveys and experiment, while in qualitative research data collection involves conducting interviews with participants and making observations (Neuman, 2009). In quantitative research, data is collected through methods, such as the number of times an incident occurs, ratings, a score a person makes on a personality test and others (Christensen et al., 2010). This study was descriptive in nature, which was more associated with qualities than it is with numbers, which is associated with a quantitative method.

The phenomenological design was selected for the current study because it was ideal and was used to provide the Kenyan immigrants in mid to senior management positions an opportunity to describe in detail personal experiences and perspectives, regarding barriers they experienced in attaining leadership positions in their respective fields. Applying a phenomenology approach indicated the study was focusing on lived experiences of the people describing the phenomena as accurately as possible (Groenewald, 2004). The phenomenology approach focuses on facts or firsthand experience of the people involved.

The case study research design was taken into consideration for this study. The case study approach is a strategy of inquiry where the researcher concentrates on a single unit or entity and sets the boundaries (Simon, 2006). In a case study research, the researcher examines in-depth a program, an event, an activity, a process, or one or more individuals (Neuman, 2009). The phenomenological design was deemed suitable because it was used to explore the Kenyan immigrants in mid to senior management positions perceptions regarding the barriers they experienced in attaining leadership positions in their organizations. The case study does not work on perception. The case study is bound by time and activity, and the data collection procedure requires extended time. A case study required more time, money, and means (Neuman, 2009), which were not available.

This phenomenological study involved interviewing 20 Kenyan immigrants in mid to senior management positions and provided an opportunity to participants to describe personal experiences with barriers they perceived prevented them from advancing to leadership positions in their organizations. Participants were allowed to share personal experiences as it relates to the phenomena under study. Using a qualitative approach for this study might create awareness of potential factors that may have contributed to barriers facing Kenyan immigrants in attaining leadership positions.

Research Questions

Research questions are used to guide studies for the kinds of data that the researcher will collect, and suggests how the researcher will be analyzing and interpreting the data that is collected (Leedy & Ormrod, 2010). This qualitative phenomenological study involved exploring lived experiences and perceptions of purposively selected participants from the Kenyan immigrants' community to better understand barriers impeding promotion opportunities to leadership positions in Northern California. The following research question guided this study:

R1: How do Kenyan immigrants in mid to senior management positions perceive and describe their experiences on barriers in attaining leadership positions?

Population Demographic

Population refers to a group of people who live in a particular place or geographical location with similar characteristics that differentiate the group from other groups (Krieger, 2012). The sample for this study consisted of Kenyan-born immigrants holding mid to senior level management positions in various organizations in Northern California. The interview questions were used to gather individual background information of participants that included the level of education, how long each participant had lived in the U.S., how long in the current position, gender, and age.

Participants selected for this study included men and women who were Kenyan immigrants living in Northern California in the United States. The selected participants were (1) first generation Kenyan-born immigrants, (2) holding mid to senior management positions in their respective organizations, (3) residing in Northern California in the United States, and (4) above 21 years old. Anyone who did not meet this selection criterion did not take part in the study.

Sampling

The sample for this study came from Kenyan immigrants holding mid to senior level management positions in various organizations in Northern California in the United States. Based on past research, the sample size appropriate for this study was 20 participants who were purposefully selected (Leedy & Ormrod, 2010; Cashman & McCraw, 1993). The selected participants helped to understand the research problem discussed in Chapter 1 and answer the research question. The sample size was appropriate because qualitative research is not concerned with the breadth of the research, but depth (Maxwell, 1998). Vishnevsky and Beanlands (2004) posited that the size of the sample is rarely predetermined, but researchers aim to include as many participants as possible to gain a comprehensive understanding of the phenomenon. The selection of a small sample size of participants is ideal for a phenomenological study because of its focus on a small number of cases. What is important is that participants have or had experienced the phenomenon under review, and data is collected until saturation is achieved.

The snowballing sampling strategy, also known as the network, chain referral, or reputational, were used in selecting participants for the current study (Neuman, 2009). To qualify for or to take part in this study, participants had to be Kenyan-born immigrants holding mid to senior level management positions in various organizations in Northern California. Participants had to be at least 21 years old because legally anyone above that age is considered an adult and eligible to sign the consent form and relevant materials. The sampling criteria also included education requirements for participants to have the ability to read and understand the purpose of the study, to sign consent forms, and to answer research interview questions comprehensively.

Selection of Participants

Selection of participants was through the Kenyan immigrants' non-profit organization located in Northern California. The non-profit organization had members from different geopolitical regions in Kenya. Referrals were also used for Kenyan immigrants who were not members of the non-profit organization but held mid to senior level management positions in their organizations. In essence, the snowball sampling strategy was used to select participants for this study (Neuman, 2009).

The selection of participants was also based on the Kenyan immigrants in mid and senior management positions willingness to participate in this study. Participants were contacted directly through the email, telephone, and face-to-face contacts. Participants were selected without coercion, and informed that taking part in the study was voluntary and that they could withdraw or ask to be removed from being part of the study at any given time before, during, or after the interview (Neuman, 2009). No explanation would be required or sought regarding the decision to withdraw from participating in this study.

Informed Consent

Informed consent is a statement that is used to explain the nature of a study to participants asking for voluntary agreement to participate in a study before it begins (Koh, Goh, Yu, Cho, & Yang, 2012; Neuman, 2009). Neuman (2009) posited that there be no coercion into participating, that it must be voluntary, and that participants have a right to know what the research is about to make an informed decision. The United States Department of Health and Human Services (DHHS) created some general guidelines in regards to informed consent that requires explaining to individual participants that the study will involve research, the purpose of the research study, expected duration the research will take, and the procedures or steps to be followed in the research (Koh et al., 2012). Participants must be aware of any foreseeable risks or any discomforts that may be experienced, possible benefits to participants or others in the study, the appropriate alternatives, issues of participants confidentiality, compensation if any, contact information, and participation is voluntary (Koh et al., 2012).

Participants in the current study were provided with a detailed explanation about the study and requested to sign a consent form the day of the interview. Statements contained in the consent form included

    1) identification of the researcher;

    2) the purpose of this study and the procedure;

    3) the duration of this study, or amount of time required for this interview;

    4) a guarantee their identity will remain anonymous and confidential;

    5) participation will be voluntary, and it could be terminated at any given time before or during the interview by stating the intent not to start or continue with the interview; and

    6) potential benefits of the interview, and the study to the participants (Neuman, 2006, p. 136).

The consent form (see Appendix C) provided an explanation that the information being sought and provided during the interview would remain confidential. Participants' actual names would remain confidential, and no one will have access to the data that is associated with this study (Wiles, Crow, Heath, & Charles, 2008). The importance of confidentiality was verbally reiterated during the interview, even though it was stated in the consent form. Participants were promised the study results would remain confidential (Wiles et al., 2008). To ensure participants responded openly and without reservations, participants were assured that responses and identities would remain anonymous, and confidential. Codes were assigned to conceal participants' real identity.

The consent form also emphasized that participating in this study was voluntary and that at any given time before, during, or after, and for any reason, participants had the right to stop or request to withdraw from the study, terminate the interview, or request exclusion from the study (Neuman, 2009). For additional questions or concerns after the interview, participants were provided with an email and phone number for contact. Participants were also informed that consent forms, interview notes, audio-recorded interviews, transcribed notes, and any relevant information, or material would be securely stored in a bank safety deposit box and then destroyed after three years to maintain confidentiality. Forms and notes will be shredded or burned and audio-recording interviews deleted and properly destroyed.

Participants who wished to withdraw from this study after data had been collected would use email or phone number provided and request removal from the study. Names of withdrawn participants and relevant information will be re-

moved from the list, and willing participants added as re-
placements. Any information provided by the removed participants will be deleted from the contents of the study to
ensure anonymity and confidentiality was maintained. Forms
filled during the interview and notes taken will be shredded
or burned. The audio record of participants' interview will be
deleted and destroyed.

Confidentiality

Confidentiality means that researchers have a moral obli-
gation to protect those who are studied, will hold research
data confidential, or will keep it a secret from the general
public (Lowman & Palys, 2007; Neuman, 2009). Researchers and all institutions are morally and ethically obligated to maintain or safeguard the privacy of participants in a
study and keep data information confidential (Beskow et al.,
2012; Papanikitas, 2011). Researchers should not release any
information that could link specific individuals to specific responses (Neuman, 2009; Shuchman, 2014). Neuman (2009)
posited that researchers are aware of each participant's identity and information, but are ethically and morally obligated
to keep it in confidence. Confidentiality affords participants
control over personal information and demonstrates trust and
integrity in a researcher - participant relationship (Yu, 2008).
To keep the promise of confidentiality, researchers are encouraged to use pseudonyms or codes instead of participant's
real names (Shuchman, 2014). Any information that could be
potentially used to identify study participants during the research process would not be disclosed (Wiles et al., 2008)

In this study, participants were assured that personal background information, lived experiences, and perception will

remain private and confidential (see Appendix B). Shuchman (2014) argued that, without a reliable promise of confidentiality, the free flow of accurate and pertinent information would dry up. Palys and Lowman (2006) contended that it is important to maintain strict confidentiality because it creates the foundation of trust and rapport, which enables researchers to collect data that is valid to promote the understanding of human experiences or condition. Participants will not share sensitive information if researchers are not trusted, and this action will diminish the value of research to society (Palys & Lowman, 2006). To gain participants trust and confidence, codes were assigned to conceal their real identity and to facilitate the free flow of information. Participants were assured that signed informed consent form, demographic information, audio tapes, interview notes, and all confidential materials with individual participant's information, will be securely stored in a bank safety deposit box and then destroyed after three years to maintain confidentiality

Geographic Location

The study was conducted in Northern California in the United States of America. The population for the current study consisted of Kenyan immigrants who resided in Northern California. Northern California was structurally diverse with Kenyan immigrants from different geopolitical regions. No attempt was made to expand or include participants selected from Southern California or neighboring states. The study involved participants, who were mainly from Kenya in mid to senior management positions, who lived and worked in Northern California.

Instrumentation

A research instrument (see Appendix A) was designed and used to collect face-to-face interview data for this phenomenological research study (Christensen et al., 2010). The research instrument contained a set of open-ended interview questions designed to elicit the Kenyan immigrants in mid to senior management positions' lived experiences and perceptions regarding the barriers they experienced in attaining leadership positions in their organizations. The designing of interview questions was guided by the objective of this study, and the research question. The semi-structured interview instrument was deemed as the most appropriate and ideal for this study. Interview questions were used to provide an opportunity for selected participants to offer information freely and in detail on lived experiences and perceptions.

The interview questions that were used in this study were developed using the literature review and with the assistance of three experts in the field of leadership (Merriam, 2009). These three experts were mentors for dissertations and were practitioners in their fields of specialization. The experts were also satisfied that the interview questions addressed the topics covered by the research questions.

Data Collection

Ochieng (2009) posited that, the qualitative researcher is regarded as a primary instrument for collecting and analyzing data. A qualitative researcher in the field can absorb all sources of information using all senses, noticing what is seen, heard, or touched (Neuman, 2009). The researcher is regarded as the key person in obtaining data from participants and facilitating interaction where they share rich data regarding their experiences and life world (Chenail, 2011). Qualitative research also involves choosing participants who will provide the information regarding lived experiences and perceptions of the phenomenon under review (Bernard, 2013; Neuman, 2009). This qualitative phenomenological study elicited experiences and perceptions of the Kenyan immigrants in mid to senior management positions in regard to barriers they experienced in attaining leadership positions in their organizations.

In this qualitative research study, interview questions were carefully worded to facilitate data collection from participants (Neuman, 2009). Participants were allowed to comprehensively answer interview questions without any interruption. Locke, Silverman, and Spirduso (2010) posited that collecting qualitative data takes time, and conducting quick interviews is not likely to be helpful in gaining a better understanding. Participants in the present study were encouraged to take time, freely share lived experiences and perceptions without undue influence or control from anyone. The interview questions were useful in fulfilling the aim of exploring the issue of barriers experienced by Kenyan immigrants in attaining leadership positions in their organizations.

The data collection process for the present study involved conducting face-to-face and one-on-one interviews, digital recording of interviews, taking notes and observing 20 Kenyan immigrants purposefully selected (Leedy & Ormrod, 2010) from Northern California. Participants were recruited through the Kenyan immigrants' non-profit organization located in Northern California in the United States. Potential participants were contacted through the email or telephone and requested to participate (see Appendix D). The purpose of the current study was explained to potential participants, and those who accepted all conditions were selected. The interviews were scheduled to take place at a nearby reserved library room or a rented room (see Appendix E) or any other quiet place that was convenient to participants. Participants in this study were informed that participation was voluntary, and it could be withdrawn before, during, and after the interview. Their identities would remain confidential and will not be disclosed to any outside party. The interviews required 45 to 60 minutes to complete.

In preparation for data collection process, a general conversation with individual participants was held to create at ease atmosphere before the beginning of the interview. The data collection process included

- holding a general conversation and making each participant at ease or comfortable to share individual experiences,
- signing the consent form and relevant items,
- conducting interviews in a private secure room or area to minimize interruptions or distractions,
- stating the interview timeframe to ensure there is enough time to complete the interview,
- informing participants that their actual names and interview responses will remain confidential. Use of codes will be selected to protect identity,
- making participants comfortable throughout the interview process,
- showing materials used, which will include audio recorder, written interview questions, and a notebook to record responses, and
- using the audio recorder to transcribe participant's re-

sponses as well as notes taken during the interview.

On the day of the interview, participants received a document describing the purpose of this study, researcher's contact information just in case they had any concerns or questions about the study. The information participants received included informed consent form (see Appendix C) that provided information on participants' rights, information that participation was voluntary, and the time frame it will take to complete the interview. The form also indicated the potential risks to the participants, how their identity will be kept confidential, and that data will be securely kept in a bank safety deposit box for three years before it's destroyed. The signature on the form indicated participants were above 21 years old, and permission had been granted voluntarily to serve as a participant in the current study as described. The interview process began after potential participants had signed the consent form. If potential participants did not sign the consent form, the interview did not take place. These participants were thanked for considering to participle in the current study.

At the beginning of the interview, an audio recorder was set up after participants agreed to it. The interview took place in a quiet setting (Georgi, 2006) to allow audio recording and avoid distractions. Participants provided answers to open-ended interview questions using the data collection instrument listed in Appendix A. To ensure that participants went through the same process and were asked all the same questions, the interview protocol in Appendix F was followed. Data collected from the interview was transcribed and imported to NVivo 11 qualitative research software for analysis

(QSR International, 2016). The data collected was securely kept in a bank safety deposit box for three years before it is destroyed.

Data Analysis

Data analysis involves collecting open-ended data based on the interview questions and developing an analysis using information provided by participants (Silverman, 2010). The analysis includes compiling, verifying, ordering classifying and interpreting data (Sharan, 1998). The purpose of data analysis is to answer research questions and achieve objectives of the researcher (Neuman, 2009). According to Sorensen (2008), the use of electronics devices has made it easier for researchers to use in analyzing qualitative data and code it as themes are discovered. For the current research study, face-to-face interviews were conducted with the study participants (Christensen et al., 2010). The interviews were audio recorded and notes of the participant's responses taken.

All data collected for the current study went through a phenomenological analysis using the method developed by Hursell and was modified by Moustakas (1994). The methodology strategy included reading all transcriptions to have a general idea of responses, creating a connection between the participants interviews and then selecting the responses from each description, sentence, and phrase that is relevant to the phenomenon under investigation. The phenomenological approach also included the interview data that was collected from participant responses and conversations. The data needed reviewing and analyzing and, as a result, the Van Kaam method was used for analysis. The Van Kaam's seven steps process are designed to assist researchers in analyzing participants' interview information in a systematic manner (Moustakas, 1994). The method provides a systematic procedure to analyze the collected data. The seven steps include

1. the listing and preliminary grouping;
2. reducing and eliminating;
3. clustering and thematizing the invariant constituents;
4. final identification of the invariant constituents and themes by application;
5. using the relevant, validated invariant constituents, and themes, construct for each co-researcher an individual textual description of the experience;
6. constructing for each co-researcher an individual structural description of the experience; and
7. constructing for each participant a textural-structural description of the meaning and essences of the experience (Moustakas, 1994, pp. 120-121).

The first step in analyzing data or filtering using the Van Kaam method included listing and grouping expressions and accounts of lived experiences of the Kenyan immigrants. The second step involved reduction and elimination of unrelated information, and in the third step, invariant constituents were clustered into core themes. The fourth step involved validating themes against participants' complete record (Moustakas, 1994). The fifth step involved the use of relevant themes that were validated to construct individual textual descriptions based on uncovered experiences and perceptions. The sixth step involved the construction of respondents' descriptions of individual experiences. The seventh step was the last step of filtering process and was used to create final deduced themes and meanings of the Kenyan immigrants' lived experiences. The NVivo 11 qualitative research software was used to manage, classify, sort, and arrange interview data for analysis (QSR International, 2016). NVivo 11 qualitative research software was used to assist in the analysis of text-based data through conducting rapid searches as well as line-by-line coding (QSR International, 2016). Line coding process involved organizing materials into manageable chunks or specific segments of text before establishing the meaning to the information (QSR International, 2016). Coding involved taking the text data that was collected during data collection process, dividing sentences or paragraphs into categories, and labeling each with a word or group of words that were used in the actual language of participants (Silverman, 2010). NVivo 11 software allowed coding, combining, and linking of themes to support the interpretation of the data (QSR International, 2016). In essence, the software was used to identify trends in the data and cross examining information using its search and query functions.

Reliability and Validity

Reliability means dependability or consistency of the research, and that the same thing will occur when repeated under identical or similar conditions (Golafshani, 2003; Neuman, 2009). Reliability, in qualitative research, indicates that a particular approach will be consistent across different researchers, on different projects, and it can be replicated (Neuman, 2009). Reliability is used in reference to whether scores of items on a given instrument are internally consistent, stable, and consistent (Bailey, 2006) in test administration and scoring. An instrument containing fewer errors is termed as more reliable.

To ensure reliability in a qualitative research study, examining trustworthiness is important because the strength of qualitative research is based on trustworthiness. Beck (2009) explained that trustworthiness is supported by authenticity, confirmability, credibility, dependability, and transferability of the research. Authenticity refers to the researcher's fairness in describing participant's experiences. Confirmability attests that the findings, interpretations, and recommendations are supported by data. Credibility is the believability of findings. Dependability refers to the stability or consistency of findings in different contexts and over time. Transferability refers to the ability to transfer findings to other contexts (Beck, 2009; Marshall & Rossman, 2011). The following explanations in the current study supported the trustworthiness of the research.

Reliability problems in this qualitative research may potentially arise from respondents not clearly understanding the way the questions were asked. To achieve reliability, this study used open-ended questions strategy, which allowed probing into participants' responses to ensure responses provided were consistent throughout the interview process (Bailey, 2006). To increase the level of reliability, interview questions were repeated when not sure the respondent understood the questions, and also to verify answers provided by reading back the answers to the respondent.

To further ensure reliability, the interviews were recorded using an audio-recording device to minimize misinterpretation or distortion of participant's responses. The audio-recording device captured the actual responses of participants and reduced data distortion during analysis (Gardner, 2008).

Data reliability was improved further by subjecting the research instrument to pilot testing (Chenail, 2011). Using the actual interview questions, a pilot test was conducted before the main research study. One Kenyan immigrant in mid and one in senior management positions were selected to take part in a pilot test. Participants in a pilot test followed the same procedure as the actual interview process. Participants were contacted and requested to take part in the pilot test. Participants were scheduled for the pilot test and to sign a consent form. The test took approximately 45 to 60 minutes. The data that was collected from the pilot test was normally processed, analyzed, and interpreted according to the objectives of the present study. The results of the pilot test were used to make adjustments or re-wording of interview questions in preparation for actual data collection (Chenail, 2011). The two people who were selected for the pilot test were not included in participating in the actual or main study.

Validity suggests truthfulness or how well an idea or the findings fit with reality (Neuman, 2009; Simon, 2006). In a qualitative research approach, validity means that the researcher will check for the accuracy of the research findings by employing certain procedures (Golafshani, 2003). The concern of validity is the meaningfulness of research components and whether it measures what is intended (Drost, 2011). The concern of validity in qualitative research is its authenticity, meaning that participants will give a fair, honest, and well-balanced account of social life as it was lived (Neuman, 2009). The use of the term validity has multiple meaning in this study. The term validity may mean internal validity or external validity, and to distinguish between the two, an explanation is provided below;

Internal Validity: The meaning of internal validity is that no errors are inside the design of the research project (Neuman, 2009). Internal validity deals with possible errors that may arise from participants' expressions. Neuman (2009) provides an example that, during an experiment of reasoning, participants may become sleepy or bored, and, as a result, have a lower score. In qualitative research findings, the researcher must be prepared to make valid conclusions if anything threatens the results. For this study, any arguments that occurred during the interview were noted and interpreted appropriately to ensure the findings were valid.

In a qualitative research study, internal validity may be compromised or threatened by researcher bias. Neuman (2009) indicated that the researcher might try to be objective, but non-verbal expressions can potentially influence participant's answers. To minimize the threats of bias in this study, personal perceptions regarding barriers experienced by Kenyan immigrants in mid to senior management positions in attaining leadership positions in their organizations were concealed and bracketed (Hein & Austin, 2001; Moustakas, 1994). Bracketing is a deliberate effort to stay neutral and avoid taking a position for or against the phenomenon under study (Neuman, 2009).

Moustakas (1994) indicated that it is important to avoid or exclude personal biases, perceptions, or feelings that could potentially influence a participant's responses. The researcher in a qualitative study can be the greatest threat to trustworthiness (Chenail, 2011). To address the issue of bias, a pilot test was conducted as a way of checking the research instrument. The pilot test allowed checking all interview questions responses, re-word or re-scale any questions, shorten or revise questions, assess and interpret responses and, identify any ambiguities or bias (Chenail, 2011).

External Validity: External validity refers to the ability to generalize experimental findings to events and settings outside the experiment itself (Neuman, 2009). Validity is used to address the question when something happens among a particular group of participants, whether the findings can be generalized to the general public or population (Drost, 2011; Neuman, 2009). This study did not generalize the results but provides lived experiences of 20 Kenyan immigrants in mid to senior management positions in Northern California who it was presumed represent lived experiences of Kenyan immigrants living in the United States adequately.

Summary

The discussion in Chapter 3 provided the reader detailed description of methods and design of this research study. Explored in this study were the lived experiences and perceptions of Kenyan immigrants in mid to senior management positions to better understand barriers impeding promotion opportunities to leadership positions in Northern California. The discussion included the design appropriateness in relation to the purpose statement, research questions guiding this study, and the population demographic. The chapter also included sampling procedures, informed consent, confidentiality, geographic location of this study, instrumentation, data collection strategies, applied data analysis strategies, reliability, and validity. Chapter 4 provides a detailed discussion, and analysis of the research results in this qualitative phenomenological study.

Chapter 4
Presentation and Analysis of Data

■ This chapter begins with the study's research question, the pilot test, the data collection process, and demographic information on study participants. A detailed data analysis procedure that includes participants' responses, findings of the study and themes are presented in this chapter. The chapter concludes with a summary of the discussion contained in the chapter.

The purpose of this qualitative phenomenological research study was to explore the lived experiences and perceptions of Kenyan immigrants in mid to senior management positions to better understand barriers impeding promotion opportunities to leadership positions in Northern California. The lived experience of 20 Kenyan immigrants was explored to answer the research question. Chapter 4 presents a report of the data collected in the current study and a detailed description of the data analysis process. The chapter begins with the study's research question, the pilot test, the data collection process, and demographic information on study participants. A detailed data analysis procedure that includes participants' responses, findings of the study and themes are presented in this chapter. The chapter concludes with a summary of the discussion contained in the chapter.

The focus of the current study was on personal experiences of Kenyan immigrants who occupied mid to senior level management positions in their organizations. This group of immigrants shared personal experiences and perceptions of barriers they perceived prevented them from attaining leadership positions in private and public organizations in Northern California. In-depth interviews using open-ended and semi-structured questions enabled participants to share their experiences and perceptions on barriers they were confronted with in attaining leadership positions. For accuracy, a Philips digital voice recorder was used to capture participants' verbatim responses which were later transcribed within 48 hours. Transcription of the digital files was done manually to identify emerging themes. The Van Kaam's seven-step process developed by Hursell and modified by Moustakas (1994) facilitated the phenomenological reduction and exploration of gathered data. Direct quotes were used to give weight to participants' stories. To ensure that confidentiality was maintained, codes were assigned to represent participants' names.

Research Questions

The first and necessary step in conducting successful research is formulating or developing interesting research questions (Alvesson & Sandberg, 2011; Haynes, 2016; Lipowski, 2008; Malhotra, 2013; Voss, 2003). The best way to formulate research questions is through spotting or identifying gaps in existing literature that need to be filled (Alvesson & Sandberg, 2011; Malhotra, 2013). The aim of developing research questions is to make a significant contribution to the body of knowledge and not for the sake of research (Haynes, 2016; Voss, 2003). Lipowski (2008) indicated that research question is a statement that requires to be explored further, and it is indeed the purpose of the study that is stated in a form of a question.

The present study adopted a qualitative phenomenological approach and focused on one research question. The study explored the lived experiences of Kenyan immigrants in mid to senior management positions to find out what they perceive as barriers to advancement to leadership positions in their organizations in Northern California. Data collection and analysis addressed the following research question:

> **R1:** *How do Kenyan immigrants in mid to senior management positions perceive and describe their experiences on barriers in attaining leadership positions?*

The research question formulated for the research study and the purpose of the study was interrelated, and both originated from the study problem. The research question would direct the study to achieve the purpose of the study by concentrating the research process on obtaining, and analyzing rich descriptions of barriers impeding promotion opportunities to leadership positions by participants. The results might lead to suggestions on how to overcome those barriers and increases chances of attaining leadership positions. A list of interview questions appears in Appendix A.

Pilot Study

A pilot test is a trial run before the actual or main study takes place (Arain, Campbell, Cooper, & Lancaster, 2010; Leon, Davis, & Kraemer, 2011; Thabane, Ma, Chu, Cheng, Ismaila, Rios, Goldsmith et al., 2010). The purpose of performing a pilot test is to test the feasibility of the techniques, methods, questionnaires or research instrument, and the interviews and how they function or work together in a study (Cope, 2015). In essence, the pilot test is used to demonstrate or confirm that the methods and procedures can work if used on a large scale (Thabane et al., 2010). Some of the advantages of performing a pilot test include, to assess the adequacy of study methods and procedures, develop and assess the adequacy and quality of research instruments and questionnaires, assess participant recruitment strategies, identify potential problems, assess the research protocol, assess the effectiveness of sampling techniques, and assess proposed data analysis (Cope, 2015).

For the current study, the interview questions (see Appendix A) were shown to two participants, one in mid and another in senior management positions. The two participants were each given an Informed Consent Form (see Appendix C), to read, sign, and date, and a Request for Participation letter (see Appendix D). Each participant was requested to go over each interview question and explain to the researcher their understanding of the question. Each participant confirmed that they understood the interview questions perfectly and that the questions were appropriate for the purpose of eliciting a response to the research question in the current study. As a result, no adjustments were made to the interview questions. The two participants did not take part in the main study.

Data Collection Process

In the month of March 2016, after obtaining Institutional Review Board (IRB) approval from the University of Phoenix, an email was sent to the Kenyan immigrants' non-profit organization leaders in Northern California to request them to forward an email to the group members with the request for participation (see Appendix D) information soliciting their participation in the research study. Once an email was sent, 15 Kenyan immigrants holding mid to senior level management positions in Northern California replied directly to the researcher expressing their willingness to be part of the study and also seeking for more information about the study. Eight more participants were referred by other Kenyan immigrants. The purpose of the study was explained, and any concerns were addressed. A total of two potential participants failed to respond in a timely manner and were considered withdrawn. One participant was unable to take part in the study due to work related commitments.

Reiteration of research purpose, confidentiality, and data collection procedures was done through telephone and email to the 20 confirmed participants. Copies of the Informed consent form (see Appendix C) and interview questions (see Appendix A) were provided to participants in advance for familiarization and to avoid any possible stress. A follow-up telephone call was made, or email was sent a couple of days later to facilitate the scheduling of the interview date and place. All participants chose a venue that was close and convenient to them. On the day of the interview, each participant appended an ink signature on the informed consent form before answering the interview questions. This was a confirmation that each participant understood the data collection procedures and willingness to participate in the study (Leedy, & Ormrod, 2010). All participants agreed to be voice recorded.

The participants were also advised of their right to withdraw from the research study at any given time without incurring any penalty or loss of benefit. If any of the participants opted to withdraw from the research study, instructions were provided to contact the researcher through the phone number or email provided on the consent form as shown in Appendix C. Participants were advised of the steps that would be followed to keep all data and information confidential securely in a bank safety deposit box. Participants were informed that after three years, all data that was collected during the research study would be destroyed. Forms and notes will be shredded or burned and audio recorded interviews deleted and properly destroyed. Each participant was offered an opportunity to ask any last minute questions or concerns that needed to be addressed before commencing the interview for data collection. No additional questions were asked by each of the study participants.

The data collection applied the use of face-to-face interviews with study participants. Each participant's interview lasted between 45 and 60 minutes in length. Face-to-face interviews allowed for the collection of rich descriptions of data during the interview process (Moustakas, 1994). Study participants were asked a series of semi-structured, open-ended interview questions. An advantage of using open-ended questions allowed each study participant to provide detailed answers based on personal experiences and perceptions (Silverman, 2010).

During the interview process notes were taken to capture any additional information that participants may have provided but was omitted or was not captured by the digital recorder. Once each interview ended, an effort was made by the researcher to transcribe data as soon as possible preferably that evening or the next day. This ensured the accuracy of data that was collected and recorded was maintained. To further ensure the accuracy of data that was transcribed, the process was repeated at least twice or as many times as necessary. Each interview that was conducted followed the interview protocol of the research study as indicated in Appendix F. Christensen et al., (2010) noted that the interview protocol is basic instructions for the interviewer to follow as the standard procedure from one interview to another. Each study participant received a verbal explanation of the purpose of the research study.

Some of the observations that were made on interview notes were that each participant appeared to be comfortable, relaxed, and engaged during the interview process. Participants willingly provided detailed answers to each interview questions describing personal experiences and perceptions on barriers to attaining leadership positions in their respective organizations. As indicated by Christensen et al., (2010) a good investigator of a qualitative study should possess the ability to ask good questions, to be adaptive and flexible, to be a good listener during data collection, and to have a clear understanding of the social phenomenon being studied.

Table 2
1. Summation of Demographics

Participant Code	Years in the US	Position or Title	Years in position	Education	Gender	Age	Industry
1a	20	District Manager	1	MA	M	41	Retail
2a	15	Sr. Manager	2.5	BSc.	M	41	Financial Services
3a	19	Project Manager	51/2	MBA	F	40	Management Consulting
4a	36	Distribution Manager	20	BSc.	M	65	Appliances and Logistics
5a	6	Operations Supervisor	1	Diploma	M	39	Materials and Logistics
6a	17	Customer Support Manager	3	MA	M	35	Healthcare
7a	30	Senior Research Scientist	5	PhD	M	48	Biotech
8a	12	Clinical Supervisor	4	MPH	F	39	Healthcare
9a	17	Accounting Supervisor	4	MSc	M	44	News Media
10a	9	Lead Network Engineer	4	BSc.	M	42	Networking
11a	11	Director of Revenue	31/2	BSc, CPA	M	41	Information Technology
12a	17	Office Manager	2	MBA	M	46	Education
13a	11	Senior Manager SEC	6 months	BSC, CPA	M	42	Financial Services
14a	21	Communications Director	3	MJ	M	41	News Media
15a	36	House Manager	12	MA	F	62	Healthcare
16a	29	Financial Manager	15	MBA	M	52	Local Government
17a	11	Corporate Controller	3	BSc, CPA	M	46	Semi-Conductor
18a	11	Senior Director	21/2	BSc, MBA, CPA	M	46	Solar Industry
19a	28	Site Manager	3	PhD	M	51	Education Agency
20a	26	Senior IT Manager	2	MBA	F	45	Pharmaceutical

Demographic Information on Study Participants

The introductory section of the research instrument sought to gather personal background data about the participants (see Appendix A, *page 247*). The introductory questions were used to gather individual background information of participants that included how long each participant had lived in the U.S., how long in the current position, type of organization, the level of education, gender, and age. To meet the selection criteria for the study, the sample of participants was required to be composed of (1) first generation Kenyan-born immigrants, (2) holding mid to senior management positions in their respective organizations, (3) residing in Northern California in the United States, and (4) above 21 years old. Table 2 provides a synopsis of the demographic data.

As indicated in Chapter 3, the 20 study participants were identified using a purposive sampling approach. Purposive sampling was a process where study participants are selected because they met the selection criteria and were willing to participate in the study (Cashman & McCraw, 1993; Christensen et al., 2010; Leedy, & Ormrod, 2010). Christensen et al., (2010) recommended purposeful sampling in qualitative studies because this type of sampling allowed the researcher to identify individuals who possessed rich pieces of information regarding the social phenomenon under investigation. In essence, selecting participants that will best help in understanding the problem and the research question.

2. Years in the United States (Northern California) and Visa Type

Participants' duration of stay in the United States ranged from 6 years to 36 years (see Table 2). Participants came to the United States under different visa categories that included students, professional workers, legal permanent residents, and visitors. Most of the participants (60%) came to the U.S. in search of academic opportunities and ended up staying for various reasons. Those who came to the U.S. as professional

or skilled workers accounted for 20% of participants interviewed. The legal permanent residents were 15%, and one
participant (5%) came in as a visitor but converted into a student and later legal permanent resident (Table 3).

Table 3
Years in the U.S.

Visa Type	n	%
Student	12	60
Professional or Skilled worker	4	20
Legal Permanent Resident	3	15
Visitor	1	5

3. Outline of Participants' Industry or Type of Organization

The Kenyan immigrants interviewed for this study were in
more than eight different industries in Northern California.
Seven (35%) of the Kenyan immigrants interviewed were
providing financial services for their organizations. Some of
the industries represented by participants included retail,
management and consulting, manufacturing and distribution,
healthcare, education, customer service and information and
communication technology (Table 4, *next page*).

Table 4

Outline of participants' industry or type of organization

Type of industry	n	%
Retail	1	5
Financial Services	7	35
Management and Consulting	1	5
Manufacturing and Distribution	2	10
Healthcare	3	15
Education	2	10
Customer Service Support	1	5
Information and Communication Technology (ICT)	3	15

4. Years in Position and Service

Respondents' length of service in current positions in their organizations ranged from 6 months to 20 years with an average of 4.8 years. The summation of demographics in figure 2 (*next page*) shows participants who have been in their current management positions between 6 months to 5 years were sixteen (80%), between 5 to 10 years was one (5%), between 11 and 15 were two (10%) and sixteen and above was one (5%).

Participants who have been in the same organization for more than ten years accounted for 30% (1a, 4a, 7a, 9a, 15a, and 19a) of those interviewed. Those who indicated that they have held management positions either in the same organization or different organizations were 35% (1a, 11a, 13a, 17a, 18a, 19a, and 20a). One participant (19a) indicated that he had been given a promotion, and he was in the process of preparing to assume a new position in a couple of months after training and handing over his site to the new manager.

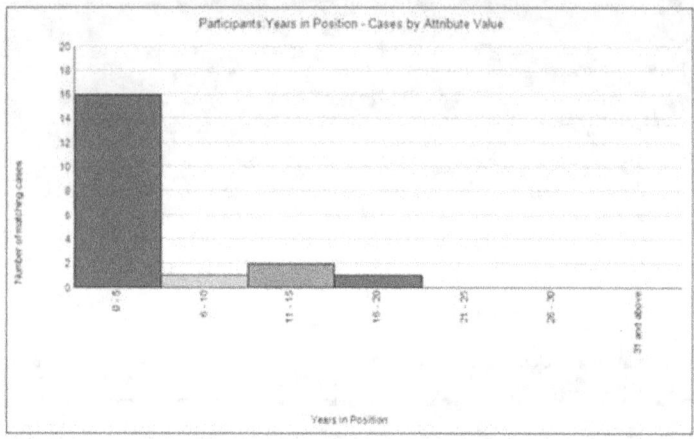

Figure 2: Years in position and service

5. Participants' Level of Education

Participants' highest level of education was comprised of a diploma, bachelors, masters and doctorate degree levels (see Figure 3). One participant had a diploma (5%), seven participants had a bachelor's degree (35%), ten participants had a master's degree (50%), and two participants had a doctorate degree (10%). Some participants also had various certifications such as certified public accounting (CPA) and registered nursing. Some participants indicated that they were pursuing further academic opportunities and other specialized certifications that are necessary for their jobs. The types of degrees and certifications sought were directly linked to their area of interest.

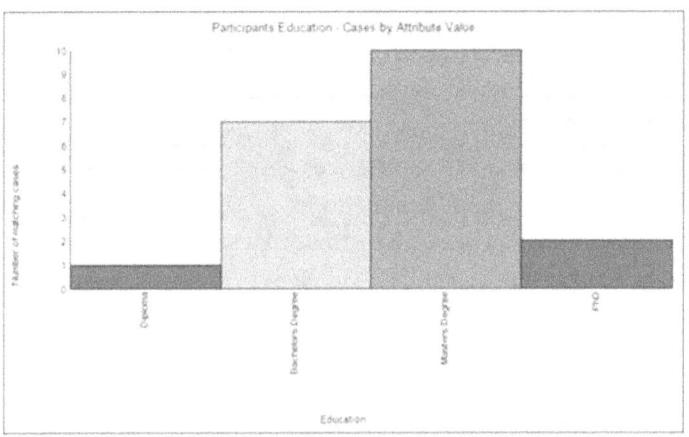

Figure 3: Participant's level of education

6. Age and Gender of Participants

The research instrument revealed that all participants in mid to senior level management positions were above the age of 35 years old (see Table 2, *page 118*). The instrument also revealed 15% of participants were below the age of 40, those in the age bracket of 40 and 49 were 65%, between 50 and 59 were 10%, and between 60 and 69 were 10%. The number of women participating in the study was 20%, while men accounted for 80% of participants interviewed. Overall, the study indicated that the majority of participants (65%) in mid to senior level management positions were concentrated between the age of 40 and 49.

7. Open-Ended Interview Questions

The interviews were conducted between April 1, 2016, and May 22, 2016, with each lasting between 45 and 60 minutes and consisted of 15 open-ended questions (Appendix A). Before the interview, a few minutes were taken to hold a general conversation with each participant to establish some rapport. Each interview session began with a brief explanation of the purpose and details of the interview procedure. It was emphasized that there were no right or wrong answers, and these gave participants the flexibility to freely share their experiences. Participants were also provided a signed confidentiality statement (see Appendix B, *page 249*) that indicated that the information provided will remain confidential and will not be shared by anyone. The consent form was also explained, and each participant signed it before the interview began. Each participant demonstrated enthusiasm about the study and anticipation for the findings. Some requested to be informed about the outcome.

Data Analysis Procedure

The goal of data analysis for the current research study was to sift through the rich description of data collected from study participants during the interview process and coding the data into themes. Saturation of data was sought and included comparing data until no new or additional information or themes were developed. Silverman (2010) noted that data collection and analysis during qualitative research occurs simultaneously. While there was more than one way of performing data analysis in qualitative research, the Van Kaam's method developed by Hursell and modified by Moustakas (1994) was used to analyze data gathered from participants in the interview process. The NVivo 11 software (QSR International, 2016) was used in the labeling, organizing, and coding of collected data that resulted in the following themes: (a) Networking, (b) social environment, (c) leadership process,

(d) economic environment, (e) culture, (f) organizational politics, and (g) discrimination.

All data that were collected for this study went through a phenomenological analysis using the Van Kaam's seven steps method developed by Hursell and modified by Moustakas (1994). The steps assisted in analyzing participants' interview information in a systematic manner (Moustakas, 1994). The method provided a systematic, organized, and orderly procedure to analyze the collected data. The Van Kaam's seven steps included listing and preliminary grouping, reduction and elimination, clustering and thematizing, final identification and validation, fundamental textural and structural descriptions, individual textural descriptions, and final deduced themes or findings.

Listing and Preliminary Grouping

In listing and grouping expressions and accounts of lived experiences of the Kenyan immigrants, all statements were treated as having equal value; a process known as horizonalization. The result of horizonalization was the derivation of "textural meanings and invariant constituents of the phenomenon" (Moustakas, 1994 p. 90). To achieve accuracy, the voice recorded conversations were listened to several times and the redundant text was removed leaving only the textual constituents. All data were manually transcribed. Visually reading the transcripts, replaying specific excerpts, and rereading passages as considered necessary clarified the expressions.

Reduction and Elimination

In reduction and elimination process, participants' statements that were relevant to the study objective were abstracted and labeled (Moustakas, 1994). Statements that were irrelevant to the study, those repetitive, vague, and overlapping were deleted or presented in more descriptive terms. The remaining statements became the invariant constituents of the experiences. Phenomenological reduction offered an opportunity to construe the participants' subjective experiences; taking meaning expressed at face value.

Clustering and Thematizing

The clustering and thematizing process involved organizing the invariant constituents into themes to develop a textural description of the barriers phenomenon (Moustakas, 1994). The NVivo 11 data analysis software was used for organizing and managing files and researcher field notes containing the filtered participants' accounts and experiences (QSR International, 2016). Highlighted words and ideas of each participant provided code labels for the blocked text.

Final Identification and Validation

The final identification and validation step involved checking the invariant constituents against the transcriptions for explicitness and consistency (Moustakas, 1994). Compound matrix queries searched for variation in structure, themes, and meaning. A return of null values signified the meaning was consistent, thus validating the meaning of the invariant constituents.

Fundamental Textural and Structural Descriptions

The consistent derivations facilitated creation of individual fundamental textural and

Structural meaning and essences of the barriers experience (Moustakas, 1994). Intuitive integration of the participants' words, responses, opinions, and quotes, resulted in a unified statement. The combined accounts facilitated a deeper understanding of the barriers phenomenon in attaining leadership positions in Northern California.

Individual Textural Descriptions

To maintain participants' confidentiality, code names were assigned in place of participants' real names (See Appendix G). The objective of the interviews was to understand how the barriers phenomenon is interpreted and navigated by the Kenyan immigrants in mid to senior level management positions in private and public organizations in Northern California. A description of each participant's experience was constructed using excerpts from the transcripts and explained in detail as provided below.

Participant 1a

Participant 1a came to the United States in 1996 as a student. Like any other international student, his goal was to go to school, complete his degree, get some skills, and head back to Kenya. But instead, he opted to stay longer after completing his Bachelor of Science (BSc) and Master of Science (MSc) degree to assist his family. Participant 1a indicated that he had a rough time when he arrived in the United States 20 years ago. Adjusting to the new environment away from family and friends was a major challenge. Language issues and making new friends was also a challenge. But as time went by he was able to adapt and managed to survive. The participant said;

It is tough coming from a third world country. I did not have a social background and the things that I went through. I had to adapt to the new environment, and I had to change otherwise I will not succeed. I had to be open-minded and willing to adapt. I had to be open to change to succeed in this country (Participant 1a).

Participant 1a has held several management positions in the same organization for the past 13 years. He is currently a district manager in charge of 16 retail stores in Northern California. This participant encountered cultural, social, political and economic barriers in his organization and so far he has been able to obtain some promotions. These promotions were attributed to hard work, being a team player, producing expected results, networking, and adapting to organizational changes. To obtain leadership positions participant 1a said;

I have to know management, and they have to know me. Otherwise, it is hard to sell myself. I must know who is up there and who will promote me. I have to work with them to know they can depend on me, they know me and when promotions come I have a chance. But producing results must be at the top. I have to be visible and defend myself. I must know people to sell myself, and must speak up to be heard (Participant 1a).

Participant 2a

Participant 2a is a senior manager at a financial services organization. He came to the United States in 2001 to pursue academic opportunities. The participant moved to Northern California four years later after completing his Bachelor's degree in accounting. He has been employed with the current organization for eight years and as a senior manager for the last two and half years. The participant's experience in migrating to the United States included culture shock. He realized that "People related to each other differently in homes or places of work, and had different perspectives on various issues. I got used to it that it is the U.S. way of life. I can do anything I want to do. I have to be focused to work toward my goals. Nothing comes easily to anybody" (Participant 2a).

Participant 2a contended that Kenyan immigrants are also disadvantaged because they are not vocal enough and come into the U.S. timid. He said that "We are timid in meetings. Speak when spoken to. Not speaking your mind in the U.S. is taken as lacking the knowledge. It takes a while for people to know your potential" (Participant 2a). It takes time and effort to make adjustments to the American way of life and to compete at the job market.

According to participant 2a, moving up the organization's chain is not easy. He said that "you have to be at the right place at the right time, build the right network, have a mentor to help move up the ranks, someone to vote for you. Raise up your hand, you need a mentor" (Participant 2a). The organization's leadership is dominated by white males who make all the decisions, while women and immigrants are in lower ranks. The participant referred the leadership as old boys' network club which is difficult to break. To rise up the ranks, participant 2a said that, "everything is performance based. You have to work very hard. You have to do more than the person sitting next to you, and nothing is handed to you" (Participant 2a). When asked about the economic environment, participant 2a indicated that the U.S. economy and the financial health of the organization play a significant role in attaining leadership positions. The participant said that;

> Not too much business coming in at the moment. The economy impacts investment decisions and strategy of the organization. Strategic initiatives are not done at the moment because of the economic slowdown. The obstacle is not being able to hire regardless of the heavy workload. Delivering the same amount of work but cannot hire. That also means I cannot move up becomes of the economy (Participant 2a).

Participant 3a

Participant 3a came to the United States in 1997 to pursue academic opportunities after completing high school in Kenya. It was difficult for her to figure out what to major in and tough adjusting to the new environment. Being away from parents, trying to get a job and coming up with tuition was not easy. The participant completed her Bachelor's degree and later managed to complete her Master's in business administration (MBA) degree.

The participant's organization does not have the leadership process in place that employees can follow to attain leadership positions. Participant 3a indicated that the organization is small and requires everyone to work hard to maintain clients and try to extend contracts. As a project manager, she has to look for more opportunities and work hard to keep her job. She has faced many challenges in an effort to maintain her current position and to grow in the organization. Given the flat structure of the organization, this participant said that to be a leader;

> You have to show interest. It is hard to get to be the

leader. The current leaders have been there forever since the company started and I am not interested to become a leader. It is difficult seeing how long some other people who have been there longer and still not getting those positions (Participant 3a).

Participant 3a expressed no interest in becoming a leader in her organization because it is too difficult to attain, believes she is not aggressive enough, she has to work harder than everyone else, and it is difficult to balance work and family. The participant believed that her culture plays a role and as an immigrant, she is not wired to be aggressive when she said that "I am not aggressive enough. Kenyan immigrants or Africans are not wired to be aggressive" (Participant 3a). The participant said that she needs the confidence to fight, to socialize and to network. The participant is too busy at home with her family to fight and as a result, she does not have the time to attend the organization's events to build a network. She acknowledges the importance of socializing and networking when she said that;

> Business is done on those social events, help in getting to know new clients, which projects are coming in, and get good assignments. Socializing is important but I have no time. You have to be engaged but it is hard. You have to go to those meetings or events and know what is going on. Someone will remember you (Participant 3a).

Participant 4a
Participant 4a came to the United States in 1980 to go to college since at the time Kenya did not have enough to ac-

commodate everyone who had finished high school. The participant experienced many challenges when he came to the U.S., but culture shock was at the top of the list. Living with an American family while attending college was quite a challenge for the participant. It was difficult to be understood because of the accent and understand the way Americans speak. The participant completed college and decided to stay in the U.S. after securing a job.

The participant has been a logistics manager for over 20 years. He started as lead, then supervisor and then manager. To grow in the organization, participant 4a indicated that he had to work very hard for many years to help the company succeed and in return he was rewarded. The participant said that "the success of the organization is tied to the success of the individual and hard work pays" (Participant 4a). To attain leadership positions in this organization is challenging because it is performance based and people skills. To be a leader immigrants have to be patient, have people knowledge, be accommodative, good listeners and tend to employees' needs, work hard and excel in achieving organizational goals. To be a leader, participant 4a also said;

> As an immigrant, I have to prove myself beyond the other American people who were born here regardless of a college education. With the accent, people will mimic you. You will have closed doors unless you come up and prove yourself. Do not despair, work hard, and don't allow anything to kill your dreams. We have good companies here in Northern California, and there are opportunities here as well (Participant 4a).

Participant 5a

Participant 5a came to the United States in 2010 through the Diversity Visa program also known as the 'green card' which is open to people from countries that have a low population of immigrants in the United States (U.S. Department of State, 2015). He came with his family which made it difficult to manage financially even though he had some relatives in the U.S. Some of the challenges he experienced included financial hardships, language problems, communication problems, getting used to different foods, lack of transportation, and socializing. The participant posited that in Kenya it was easier to make friends, but in the U.S. it was difficult to find friends to share, and he was lonely at the beginning.

Participant 5a is currently operations supervisor which he has held for one year in a materials and logistics company. The only way for this participant to attain this position was through changing from day shift to night shift because nobody wanted the position. Participant 5a admitted that his management position came with its fair share of challenges like the American colleague's attitude towards immigrants because they believe that immigrants are supposed to be employees and not managers. The participant shared his frustrations with working at this shift because he is the only decision maker at those hours. He has to make any critical decisions and resolve any conflicts that may arise during his shift. Sometimes employees ignore his directions, imitate him, think they are better than him and are not free to be led by not only a black person but also an immigrant.

The leadership process in this organization entails correctly handling materials, understanding receiving procedures, transactions, verification process, and handling fragile parts.

Exemplary performance and understanding the business operations process may help in getting a promotion but sometimes it may not. In the past, the participant had trained some new employees who obtained management positions before he did. Attaining leadership positions in this organization may not be easy and could be very stressful. The participant asserted that there was an invisible ceiling on how far up into leadership he could go. Even to get the top management positions the participant said, "I have to work harder and perform better than everyone" (Participant 5a).

Participant 6a

Participant 6a came to the U.S. in 1999 when he was barely 18 years old to pursue academic opportunities immediately after completing high school in Kenya. He obtained an associate degree, then Bachelor's degree and later a Master's degree. The participant confesses that he had no intentions of staying in the U.S. except to earn his degree and go back to Kenya. But after he was conferred a Bachelor's degree he got a job, started a family, and it does not seem he will be leaving the country any time soon.

Participant 6a has worked in the current organization for eight years and as a customer service manager for three years. This participant shared information that the leadership process in the organization was haphazard. His management position was attributed to personal capacity that included hard work and exemplary performance. The organization does not have a clear direction nor path individuals may follow to attain leadership positions. According to participant 6a, having proper leadership process in place may lead people to attain leadership positions within their roles based on effectiveness, but that effectiveness is hard to measure in the organization given different approaches, expectations, and cultures in Silicon Valley. The participant said;

I have seen a lot of changes in the leadership level, high turnover, and new vision with every turnover. New direction, lack of direction and sometimes we are not what it is expected of us. There is a huge disconnection in the leadership level. Lack of understanding of business needs, team needs and no continues process we can all sign up to (Participant 6a).

Participant 6a indicated that the chaotic nature of the organization makes the social environment untenable. The organization hardly holds social events and as a result, employees just come to work and then go home. Considering the organization has a huge presence of immigrants' population, there is no time to socialize and to network. It is difficult to attain leadership position in this kind of environment.

Participant 7a

Participant 7a came to the U.S. in 1988 as a student with the intention to study, learn a trade, gain some experience and go back to Kenya. He pursued academic opportunities that were available to him and obtained a doctorate degree. When the participant arrived in the U.S., the first thing he recognized was the different culture. At first, the experience in the U.S. was overwhelming, huge cultural shock. He did not know what a hamburger was, was not privy to credit cards, not having had a driver's license, and not able to speak English clearly for fellow students to understand him. The expectation was also to gain employment to sustain him and as a

foreign student, there were a lot of restrictions. It was difficult to secure a job to enable him to settle down and other
challenges.

Participant 7a is currently a senior research scientist, and
his role is to oversee associates in designing drugs, designing
of molecules that could be used for potential therapeutics in
areas that the company wants to focus on. This involves
meetings either one-on-one or group discussions, looking at
data, designing avenues to address limitations on making materials or interacting with colleagues from other departments
that they collaborate with in particular projects to achieve organizational goals.

The participant posited that the leadership process in this
organization is clearly defined and it is based on which track
individuals are in. The organization has two tracks namely;
scientific and management track. He is on the scientific side
which has a ceiling how far up he could go. In order to move
beyond that ceiling, he has to move to the managerial side
which he is not interested in doing. The company does make
all those avenues available, but the participant is comfortable
where he is at. The participant mentioned that to move up is
not easy and what the organization does is to pump up the titles. It is also obvious that the number of minorities are in-
credibly few. In a department of about 200 employees, there
are only two blacks after one had left the organization, which
brings in the race factor. The participant feels that it is difficult to network in this environment when he said that;

> Networking helps in knowing what is going on in dif-
> ferent departments in an informal way which some-
> times is very useful. You get a sense of ideas where
> projects are in informal way, and ask questions which

you may not ask in normal meetings. These helps in knowing where the company is and to grow (Participant 7a).

Participant 8a

Participant 8a came to the United States in 2004 to join her husband who had come to study. When she arrived, she experienced the culture shock that all immigrants have to go through. The participant said that "it was hard talking to people and sometimes they didn't understand me because I have the accent. I had to learn how to talk, how to relate to people, and be able to blend in. I had to make an effort to adapt to the new environment" (Participant 8a). The participant was also considering going to college and she had to make the adjustments. This participant went to college and obtained Bachelor's degree and then a Master's degree two years ago.

As a clinical supervisor, this participant is in charge of coordinating patient care with nurses, families and patients. It is a fast paced environment because it involves taking care of people who have different medical conditions and needs. To be in her current position she had to be educated and receive training. The participant said that the leadership process in the healthcare industry required education, training, and experience. Having the right education and experience will make it easier to climb the organization's ladder. But the union environment in the organization can prevent someone from climbing the leadership ladder. The presence of the union means there is policies, rules, and laws' surrounding what has to be done and how it has to be done. This includes who has to be promoted and when.

Participant 9a

Participant 9a came to the United States in 1999 with a student visa immediately after completing high school in Kenya. His initial experience was pleasant because he had family members already in the U.S. who provided food, housing, transportation and tuition to attend school. The participant stated that "for two years I did nothing but go to school. The only challenge was that the food was different, the culture was different, but my family members helped me to make the necessary adjustments to the American way of life" (Participant 9a).

Participant 9a is currently an accounting supervisor in a news media organization in Northern California. In his role, the participant is required to manage the general ledger (GL), reconciliation with all payables and then I reconcile fixed assets to the GL. The participant has been with the privately owned organization for 15 years and as a supervisor for four years. He started as a clerk and became a supervisor, and he hopes to continue to grow. The only issue is that everyone working for his accounting department has been there for over ten years, and employees hardly leave except through retirement. Attaining a leadership position will definitely take a while, and the organization promotes from within and according to seniority.

The participant revealed that his organization is rigid and has a predetermined path on who gets what position based on seniority. According to the participant, "even if I acquire more education or training it will not make a difference, still I have to wait on queue patiently for my turn" (Participant 9a). For the participant to be promoted, the immediate manager has to leave the organization, get promoted, or the company creates a new position.

As for the social life, the participant joked that "what can you expect from accountants except crunching numbers" (Participant 9a). The participant revealed that social life is dead in accounting department. Everyone in the department comes to work, do their part and go home. In essence, the organization's structure and in some cases departments play a role in slowing down or hindering individual's career growth.

Participant 10a

Participant 10a migrated to the United States in 2007 after pursuing academic opportunities in the United Kingdom (U.K). After completing a Bachelor of Science degree in engineering in the UK, the participant migrated to the United States to join some family members. The participant's experience in migrating to the U.S. was not that bad considering he had his sister who helped him to settle down fairly easily. The participant also had this to say;

> It was hard finding a job, and it took me about three months. There was the culture shock, the accent, new job, and I had difficulty understanding the social scene. What people are excited about, baseball, and basically learning and getting used to the new environment. There was also getting used to office politics which was different from the U.K. In U.K. people just work and not concerned about gaining political mileage (Participant 10a).

In his organization, participant 10a is responsible for engineering networking solutions, ensuring network security is up to date in the whole organization which has about 120 locations worldwide, and to make sure it is secure at all times. To attain leadership positions in this organization is not easy because the career path is not defined. The participant says, "there is no leadership process in place in that if you work for a certain number of years you expect to be promoted. It feels like it is unachievable to get to the top level of leadership such as director and above" (Participant 10a).

Even though the organization is culturally diverse, it is still difficult to advance because common cultures tend to stick together. The politics of the organization is also a major stumbling block. No matter how the company tries to conceal or hide politics, he concedes, it happens, "the organization might not do it in your face, but if you open your eyes you will see it. To get a promotion, you have to interact with people from different cultures, you have to play the political game, and be part of certain grouping or circles" (Participant 10a).

Participant 11a

Participant 11a migrated to the United States in 2005 as a professional or skilled worker. The participant was brought into the United States with the organization he was already working for in Kenya. The experience of migrating from Kenya to the U.S. was smooth considering the sponsoring organization provided the air tickets, arranged for accommodation for a couple of months, gave a loan to buy a car, and was introduced to a bank that provided him a credit card. The participant acknowledges that he was set to succeed and did not have to go through what other Kenya immigrants went through.

The participant has been a director of revenue for three and half years, and he held other management positions before.

The role of director of revenue is to assess the organizations revenue base before even looking at the profit. An organization's revenue is an indicator of the potential for growth or how well the organization will perform in any given business deals. The participant advises various groups such as sales on what can and cannot be done from the revenue standpoint when closing business deals.

Participant 11a's company does not believe in having hierarchies, and everyone has access to the organizations upper leadership. The company's premises have open space offices and do not have corner offices for CEO or CFO, or cubicles for anyone. The organization's leadership believes in open door policy where employees' collaboration, free information sharing, and communication are encouraged. Attaining leadership in this organization will require individuals being good at what they do and having the right connections or network to assist in achieving this goal.

When it comes to organizational politics, participant 11a admitted that it is present in the organization he works for and he prefers not to play any political games. He believes that organizational politics does not add any value to the organization except self-promotion. The participant stated that;

> There are always politics and I hate politics. When there is politics in an organization I will try to find my way out. This comes from my culture on how I grew up believing that you do not blow your own horn, you just work hard and you are recognized for your efforts. People in the U.S. talk about themselves and try to sell themselves and it is called self-promotion. In Kenya this is considered as bragging which is not good (Participant 11a).

Participant 12a

Participant 12 a came to the United States in 1999 to pursue a degree of master's in business administration. Coming to the U.S. was frustrating at first when processing student paperwork but he was also fascinated with the idea of moving to a new country, and he had a lot of expectations. When the participant arrived in the U.S., he faced many challenges that included adapting to the new environment, learning the laws and rules of the U.S. which in his opinion appeared way too many. It took him a while to get used to the American culture, the food, find a job and learn how to survive.

The participant is currently working as an office manager in a school environment that falls under a non-profit organization. His role is to oversee the day to day running of the office to make sure the teachers and the dean have the support they need to do their jobs. Participant 12a contended that the leadership process is not clearly stated in this organization. "There is no coherent communication from the leadership to indicate the process that should be followed" (Participant 12a). He also thinks that there are minimum chances of him attaining leadership position in this organization because of the political environment, the social factors, and being from a different culture. He says that "sometimes people see or perceive me as different because I am an immigrant with an accent, and I may not completely fit in, or I am not a good fit" (Participant 12a). The other barrier the participant believes will play a role include the financial constraints of the organization. Leadership positions are created based on the availability of resources, and since the organization serves in a low-income area, there is a lack of resources and as a result, minimal leadership positions are created. The chances of attaining leadership positions in this organization are therefore severely limited by the economic environment.

Participant 13a

Participant 13a migrated to the United States in 2005 with a work visa or as a professional or skilled worker. Due to the failure of U.S. corporations, organizations were looking for auditors who were in short supply in order to gain the confidence of the capital market. The participant was hired in Kenya and brought in by an auditing firm. The company helped this participant to get a visa to come to the U.S. and settle by providing sign up bonus to use to buy a ticket, buy a car, and pay rent. Participant 13a had to work for the company for at least two years to avoid repaying the loan. The experience of migrating from Kenya to the U.S. was easy considering the sponsoring organization provided accommodation for a while, and he had a job to start his life in the U.S., unlike other immigrants who came with nothing.

Participant 13a is a senior manager for SEC reporting, and he has been with the current organization for six months. He was a senior manager for three years, and a manager for three years in the same company prior to joining the current organization. The participant indicated that he is committed to the organization because of the nature of the people he is working with who are professionals. The organization has invested in his development to grow and succeed in his role. The organization is small with about 1,000 employees and growing, and the atmosphere is relaxed. The culture of the organization is open communication, collaboration, relaxed, and accommodates his needs such as allowing him to work from home or report to work any time he is able to due to family obligations.

The leadership process in participant 13a's organization is not clearly defined at this time, but he feels that if opportunities became available, he could apply, and it's a question of being able to sell himself. The participant adds that sometimes there are cultural barriers that may hinder the growth of Kenyan immigrants in their organizations. He said that;

When it comes to presenting ideas, an American tend to talk big and loud giving an impression that he or she knows a lot. Kenyan culture is between confidence and pride, sometimes Kenyans tend to be slow to speak and giving an impression that they don't know, or they have no idea what is going on. What people don't realize is that Kenyans may have better ideas than them. An American person uses large terms giving an impression as being informed. Kenyans don't show off or are not aggressive enough, and this can have an impact in getting those leadership positions (Participant 13a).

Participant 14a

Participant 14a came to the United States in 1995 to pursue academic opportunities. He described the process as a very long journey and very painful. When he graduated from high school in 1993, there were about five public universities to cater for a country of 30 million people. The bar for entry into these universities was set so high, and someone had to be either very smart or rich to go to a private university and the participant was neither. First attempt to come to the U.S. failed and on the second attempt he got a student visa to come to study. He was fortunate to have an uncle in Northern California who helped in understanding the country and make the necessary adjustments to adapt and be able to settle in the U.S.

The participant completed his bachelor's degree and later obtained a master's degree in journalism. He is currently a communication director in a non-profit news media service for small ethnic minority groups that are not big enough to request for government funding. The company advocates for small Medias that are not big enough to ask for example government advertisement dollars. The company helps small media houses to create and share content among them. The participant's role is to talk and ask more small ethnic Medias to join because there is strength in numbers. It is easier to receive funding through the organization collectively than being on their own.

As for the leadership process in this non-profit organization, it is not very clear at the moment what to do to become a leader. The leaders know what they want to do, but it is not yet spelled out what the leadership process is. The participant indicated that the executive director who has been there since 1974 likes the way things are run and she is not ready to change that. The participant also indicated that he is not interested to move into leadership positions because of the nature of the organization. As a non-profit organization, he is worried if he will be around next month, leadership is not what he wants to think about if the organization is not stable. As an organization that depends on grants, he is afraid to become a leader because that means he will be responsible for making sure the organization does not run out of money. The participant does not want to be responsible if the organization fails and employees want to be paid.

Some of the barriers cited by participant 14a included stereotyping even though the organization's employees are from diverse backgrounds, unstable financial health, company politics, and lack of social life in the organization. For example, the participant's colleagues do not believe he writes the reports that he does and that bothers him. He feels his kind is not supposed to lead but follow no matter how educated or experienced he is. The unpredictable financial health of the organization is also a major concern because the participant does not want to be in a leadership position that will make him responsible if it fails. The company politics of backstabbing makes it hard to be motivated even to want to be a leader in the organization. The participant also indicated that the organization's leaders sometimes set up social events and unfortunately most of the time they do not attend and this defeats the purpose of socializing and networking. As a result, the participant does not take part in social events anymore.

Participant 15a

Participant 15a came to the U.S. in 1980 for the purpose of attending a university which were very limited in Kenya at the time. Her first experience was the cold climate on the east coast of the United States. The food was different, and she ate what was presented to her. She also noticed that people were kind, and still thinks that people in this country are kind. She completed her bachelor's degree and later a master's degree in special education.

Participant 15a has been working for the same organization ever since she moved to Northern California in 1985. The participant works at a non-profit organization and has been a manager since 2004. The participant acknowledges the fact that it took her a long time to become a manger. It was her choice to take the time to explore all departments and understand what is being done in the organization and where she can better serve. She received the training in understanding the overall operations of the organization and to grow into leadership positions. She has been offered leadership position but she is not interested, and this is what she said;

> Personally, I don't want to be a leader because it is a non-profit organization that depends on donations and fundraising. I will have to work really hard to bring in the funds the organization needs to continue to operate. That is challenging, and I don't want to do that. I have seen how the organization is run, and I am not trained or equipped to go out and raise funds which are challenging. I will need a large social network which I do not have to enable me to raise the required funds (Participant 15a).

The participant does not recommend working for a non-profit organization because the challenges are many. The economic environment is a major challenge because the organization has to pay employees, keep the facilities well equipped, take care of the residents, and make sure their needs are met and that takes money. Sometimes the organization spends more money than what is available, and it is unpredictable where the money will come from to take care of the shortfall. To work for this kind of organization the participant posited that " you have to be ready for anything, it is challenging, it keeps you alert and busy, and you have to abide by the law.

Participant 16a

Participant 16a came to the U.S. to pursue academic opportunities in 1987 and later moved to California in 1992. The participant was sponsored to come to the U.S. to study by an American, who was teaching at a private university in Kenya. The teacher who became a friend sponsored the participant by providing air ticket, housing and the initial cost of tuition. The participant attended college and worked at the same time to repay the loan. He completed nursing school and a bachelor's degree. He worked full time while attending graduate school where he obtained a Master's degree in management and finance. The participant described his experience of migrating from Kenya and settling in the U.S. as challenging, but he was able to adapt and succeed in achieving his goals.

Participant 16a is a senior financial manager in a public institution in Northern California. This participant is in charge of reviewing budgets and programs, reviewing funding, merge different funding, make sure programs that are mandated by certain federal grants or state are in place, and develop budgets for different programs and departments in the organization. Participant 16a has been in the organization for 19 years and in his current position for 15 years. The participant expressed his views that he could make more money outside the organization, but he likes the relaxed environment and the people he works with.

The leadership process in participant 16a's organization is structured or standardized on how to move from one level to the next and what is required such as tests or courses to take to fill certain positions. But the challenge is maneuvering through the networks that are in the organization. Even if individuals go through the process, the job might be given to someone else because of the connections to the hiring authorities. Basically, there is discrimination that is going on in the organization even though it is not official. One of the major barriers experienced by participant 16a is that he has been unable to advance in the organization because he is not in the right race, circle or group and lacks the appropriate social network. Even though the organization is diverse, some races are the majority, and it is difficult to maneuver through.

Participant 17a

Participant 17a migrated to the U.S. through a work visa in 2005. His migrating experience was easy because the work visa and pertinent documents were processed by the sponsoring company. The participant shared his settling experience in the U.S. as being difficult to adapt to the new environment, new culture, not knowing anybody except his wife and four-year-old son. As time went by he got used to it, started creating connections, friendships, and networks.

Participant 17a is currently a corporate controller in charge of finances of the company, keeping the books, reporting obligations that the organization has. The participant has been in this position for three years and in the organization for five years. This participant believes that he has reached the pinnacle of where he wants to be in terms of leadership. He has no interest in becoming chief finance officer (CFO) or upper leadership positions. Considering he is an immigrant, he has succeeded in climbing the management ladder faster than he had expected.

As for the leadership process in the organization, participant 17a revealed that there is a process called annual focal process that individuals go through to determine who will get promoted based on outlined merits. The organization has changed leadership over the last few years and with each new leadership comes new vision and new process. Currently, the leadership of the organization is centralization around the CEO, and there is openness, consulting on financial matters, but the participant is not part of the inner circle. Participant 17a indicated that he had faced some challenges in attaining leadership positions in his organization. He said;

> The background of the people I work with is that they are very good presenters and express themselves very well in board meetings and articulate their points when you listen to them. As an immigrant and English as a second language, it can be intimidating and challenging to compete with them. I have a point that I want to make, but I am competing with people who are at a higher level. That has an impact if that is the only thing they are looking for. But the bay area is diverse, and that makes a difference in having a chance to advance (Participant 17a).

Like every organization, participant 17a revealed that politics is common in his place of work, and it is something he is not good at. The participant indicated that "I tend not to get in the middle of it because I don't like it but for some people, it is a game in corporate America. I avoid it as much as I can and get involved only if I have to" (Participant 17a). The participant gets involved in organizational politics if it is absolutely necessary and if it will be beneficial to career development.

Participant 18a

Participant 18a came to the United States 11 years ago as a professional or skilled worker. The participant graduated from the University of Nairobi, Kenya, with a Bachelor's degree in accounting and later completed CPA - K certification in Kenya. Participant 18a was recruited by an auditing firm that was searching for auditors and was offered to migrate to the U.S. to work for the same firm. The auditing firm made all the necessary arrangements required to migrate and travel such as the Visa, air ticket, provided initial housing and the cost of settling down. The participant indicated that he came to the U.S. alone, he did not know anybody and did not know what to expect. He explained his initial experience as;

> When I arrived at San Francisco, the company sent someone to pick me up and took me to a corporate housing for a month. I spent time walking around to find out where everything was in San Jose. I had to figure out the food brands, where to get a haircut and other things. A few days later a couple of other Kenyans came to the corporate housing and we formed the friendship that is still going on (Participant 18a).

Participant 18a has been a senior director in charge of accounting and financial reporting for his organization for two and half years. He has been with the organization for five years. His department of finance is in charge of reporting filings with SEC annual filing, generating monthly financial statements for the executives, help in deal structuring that is basically working with big companies to make deals that will help in generating revenue.

The leadership process in this organization is not yet established considering it was started six years ago. The company is still young and trying to put together a structure while creating new positions. It is difficult to know where the organization is going and what is going to happen tomorrow from the economic stand point. The company has also experienced high turnovers of executives creating uncertainties. The participant says, "for every new executive we have to form new relationships with them, we have to teach them what we do and learn his or her leadership style. We form a bond but then they keep leaving, and we have to start all over again. Also, new executives tend to bring their own people along to the organization" (Participant 18a).

Participant 19a

Participant 19a came to the U.S. as a student in 1988. He went to college and had the usual challenges of trying to support him and complete studying. It was hard to find a job because of the restrictions, but he found a way of working on campus, such as cleaning dormitories to make a little bit of money and he was even able to send some money to his family in Kenya to help out. The participant indicated that he was always eager to work, and he earned more money than he was able to earn when in Kenya. The participant obtained a bachelor's degree, got a job, worked while attending college to obtain his masters thinking he was going back to Kenya. He started acquiring materials stuff like a house, got married and his immigration process started. With a family, a home and a doctorate, he feels that the U.S. is his home even though he visits Kenya as often as he can.

Participant 19a has been a site manager in different locations in the past six years but in his current location, he had been a site manager for three years. The participant indicated that he has been with the same organization in different capacities for 23 years. He has just received a promotion, and he would assume a new role this summer. The participant attributes his growth in the organization to having the skills set and experience that he brings to the organization. Having the right skills sets and relevant experience, managing the site well, knowing how to interact and react to politics, understanding organizational culture and be able to function well within it has worked in his favor. The participant also said;

> To attain leadership positions, you need mentors or somebody who will mentor you or help you to move up. Learn all aspects of the organization since they are elastic, and they can snap and hit you in the face. Know how far to push and know the boundaries of the organization and how to poke holes without breaking them. Identify allies that you can go to within the organization when you need advice and tell you when you are wrong. Identify key people who can help you achieve your goals and know that everybody has different skills set and understand who can do what and use them to create your own success (Participant 19a).

Participant 20a

Participant 20a came to the United States in 1990 with a visitor's visa. At that time, undocumented immigrants found it difficult to move forward or survive in the U.S. The participant converted into a student status, went to school and after completion, she was hired by a company that sponsored her to obtain permanent legal status. The participant later earned a master's degree in business administration. This participant is currently a senior IT project manager in charge of global projects that entails; technical infrastructure, production support, and release management for the organization. Her role is to ensure teams come together and collaborate to make sure end goals are met. She also focuses on budget, time, and resources.

Participant 20a first striking experience she clearly remembers is when she came to the U.S. was culture shock which was difficulty in adjusting to. But she later liked it because as a woman there were more opportunities in the U.S. than in Kenya. Employment areas for a woman in Kenya are limited because women are expected to be clerks and office secretaries. In the U.S. a woman can work in any industry or in any role she pleases. It is up to the individual, and there are much more choices to make.

The leadership process in participant 20a's organization is not structured or clearly stated. The participant stated that "the leadership process, unfortunately, is not in place because of things such as politics, nepotism and gender discrimination" (Participant 20a). The company is privately and family owned and the leadership is made of family members, relatives, and close family friends. Those benefiting from attaining leadership are largely family members and relatives. The leadership is also changing to a new direction and process making it harder to know what to expect. The participant also said;

> I am at a disadvantage as an immigrant, being black and a woman. The company is privately owned by people from a community that believe that a woman should be seen and not heard. When promoting, I am not their first choice because they go for their kind. I

have to let them know I am looking for a promotion, and I have to fight for myself. As someone of a lower race, I have to work ten times harder that everybody else in order to be acknowledged anywhere. And this is a challenge (Participant 20a).

Overall, participants in this study revealed that they had experienced various challenges in advancing to leadership positions. Some of the challenges included their inability to network effectively and socialize within and outside the organization in order to obtain leadership positions. The other challenges were the financial instability of the organizations some participants worked for, and a lack of structured leadership process they could follow to climb up the corporate ladder affected them. The participants also believed that their cultural background, organizational politics, and discrimination limited their chances of advancing to leadership positions.

Findings / Results

Analysis of data gathered from face-to-face interviews of 20 Kenyan immigrants in mid to senior level management positions in Northern California yielded seven primary themes. The identified themes are as follows; (a) networking, (b) social environment, (c) leadership process, (d) economic environment, (e) culture, (f) organization politics, and (g) discrimination. These themes presented in the following section assisted in answering the research question: How do Kenyan immigrants in mid to senior management positions perceive and describe their experiences on barriers in attaining leadership positions?

Middle versus Senior Managers' Perspectives

In exploring the lived experiences of Kenyan immigrants in mid to senior level management positions, two subgroups of study participants namely; middle and senior managers were used to assess potential differences in perception on the barriers phenomenon. Responses by Kenyan immigrants in middle and senior management positions did not provide varied opinions that were significant to form distinct sets of information. Each participant identified similar challenges and contributors that directly or indirectly affected growth opportunities in their organizations.

Data Management

The NVivo 11 qualitative data analysis software was used in sorting a large amount of collected data in an orderly manner (QSR International, 2016). To identify the major themes, participants' expressions were coded in nodes for classification as elements of themes and patterns within a hierarchical structure. The coded nodes were sorted and arranged in descending order. The highest 28 referenced elements were considered significant and clustered to form seven major themes.

Emerging Major Themes

The patterns derived from the invariant constituents indicated that lived experiences of the participants support the existence of the barriers phenomenon. The seven themes referenced by at least 17 participants (Table 5) are perceived to have contributed to barriers in attaining leadership positions in their organizations in Northern California. The major themes include networking, social environment, leadership process, culture, economic environment, organizational politics, and discrimination. A detailed discussion of the seven major themes was undertaken.

Table 5:
Major Themes

Participant code	Networking	Social Environment	Leadership Process	culture	Economic Environment	Organizational Politics	Discrimination
1a	x	x	x	x	x	x	x
2a	x	x		x	x		x
3a		x	x	x	x	x	
4a		x		x	x	x	x
5a		x	x				x
6a		x	x	x		x	
7a	x		x	x			x
8a	x	x	x	x			
9a		x	x				x
10a	x	x	x	x	x	x	
11a	x	x		x	x	x	
12a		x	x	x	x	x	
13a	x	x	x	x	x		
14a		x	x		x	x	x
15a			x		x		
16a	x	x		x			x
17a		x	x	x	x	x	
18a	x	x	x	x		x	
19a	x			x			x
20a	x	x	x			x	x
TOTAL	11	17	15	15	11	11	10

From the clustered counted nodes, a hierarchical visual representation of the themes was developed. Figure 4 *(next page)* shows recurrent and prevalent patterns referenced by the participants starting with the highest to the lowest. Themes with more than 21 references were considered signif-

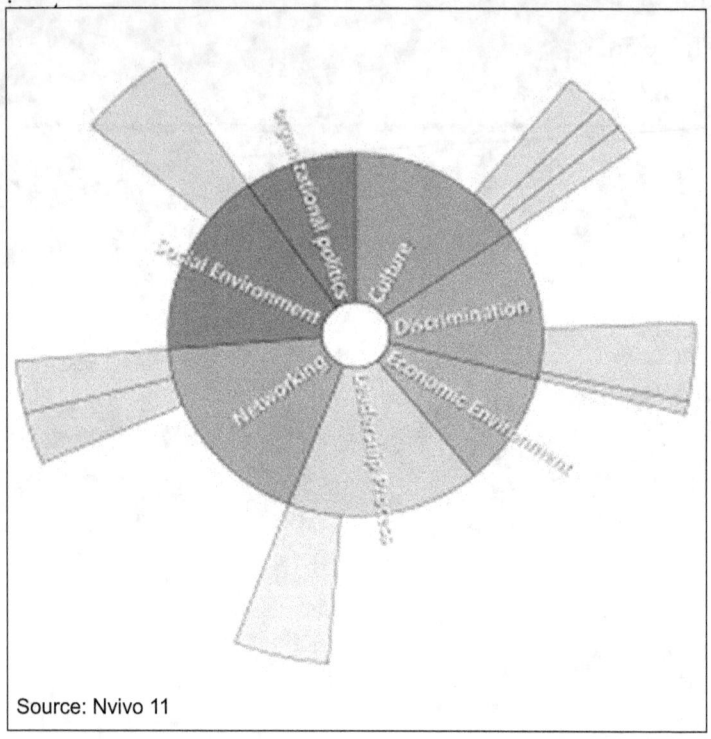

Source: Nvivo 11

Figure 4: Emergent major themes

Theme 1: **Networking**

Networking was the first major theme rated by the Kenyan immigrants in mid to senior level management positions as the barrier to attaining leadership positions in their organizations. All participants acknowledged that it is not easy for Kenyan immigrants to advance into the executive levels of leadership and that they still work very hard to maintain their current management positions. The participants described career advancement for American colleagues as being smooth and fast. Participant 17a stated that "the higher you go the fewer Kenyan immigrants you are going to find in any organization" (Participant 17a). The participants believed that for a Kenyan immigrant to become CEO of a large organization is a herculean task.

Participants in this study indicated that they lacked proper networks that would enable them to advance into leadership positions. Sixteen participants (80%) out of twenty participants referenced 28 times the lack of networks within and outside their organizations as an impediment to advancing into leadership positions. Participant 10a indicated that it is harder working in the U.S. because Kenyans do not have professional network groups like the Asians or Indians have to share, exchange, or bounce ideas. The participant continued to say that, "getting a promotion should be based on performance, but instead it depends on who you know and who knows you. Connections that you make within the organization are important" (Participant 10a). Participant 11a was in agreement when he stated that;

> To advance to executive leadership positions will be a bit of a challenge because I do not have contacts on a higher level, and I will have to fight for myself. Being an immigrant can be disadvantageous because you lack contacts or connections that can get you to leadership positions (Participant 11a).

Participant 6a, 18a, and 20a indicated that they had witnessed a CEO and top executives coming into the organization and brought people they are related to, went to school with or worked with in their previous organizations. For example, participant 18a's organization experienced high turnover of executives and he noticed that "new executives tend to bring his or her own people along to the organization" (Participant 18a). While participant 20a working at a family owned company said that "when promoting, I am not their first choice because they go for their kind" (Participant 20a). This makes it very difficult for those already in the organization to advance even if they are qualified for those positions. The Kenyan immigrants also find it challenging to maneuver through the networks that are in the organization. Participant 16a said that "Even if you go through the process, the job might be given to someone else because of the connections to the hiring authorities" (Participant 16a).

The small size of the Kenyan community in Northern California makes it more difficult to network among themselves, instead, they have to network with communities which also have their own networks. The Kenyan immigrants have to reach out to colleagues from different communities and create a network that can become useful in advancing into leadership positions. Participant 1a, 2a, 7a, and 8a posited that as an immigrant it is important to network, know more people, and connect with top management. Participant 1a said that;

> I have to know management, and they have to know me. Otherwise, it is hard to sell myself. I must know who is up there and who will promote me. I have to work with them to know they can depend on me, they know me and when promotions come I have a chance. But producing results must be at the top. I have to be visible and defend myself. I must know people to sell

myself, and must speak up to be heard (Participant 1a).

According to participant 2a, it is not easy to move up the organization's corporate ladder when he said that "you have to be at the right place at the right time, build the right network, have a mentor to help move up the ranks, someone to vote for you. Raise up your hand, you need a mentor" (Participant 2a). Participant 7a's opinion was that;

> Networking helps in knowing what is going on in different departments in an informal way which sometimes is very useful. You get a sense of ideas where projects are in an informal way and ask questions which you may not ask in normal meetings. These helps in knowing where the company is and to grow (Participant 7a).

Participant 8a believed that "the more people you know, the better network you have, the better the chances of attaining leadership positions" (Participant 8a). Networking is an essential element in attaining leadership positions in any organization. Networking helps in creating visibility and useful connections for career development.

***Theme 2:* Social Environment**

The organizations' social environment was rated as the second major theme by the Kenyan immigrants in mid to senior level management positions as a barrier to attaining leadership positions in their organizations. Fourteen (70%) participants acknowledged that participating in social activities inside and outside of the organization may assist in advancing to leadership positions, but they cited various reasons why they were not active. The reasons provided included, the organization does not have or encourage social events, the social events are held after work or only during the holidays, only attend events during work hours due to work-family conflict, and do not attend social events.

Participant 9a indicated that his organization does not have nor does it encourage social events. In a reserved manner, the participant said that "all we do is work and work and then go home. There is no social life" (Participant 9a). Even employees themselves do not hold any social events outside of work. Even though the organization's leadership does not prohibit social events, no employee has taken the initiative to set up one. Even those organizations that have social events, such as participant 14a's company, "the leaders do not always come to these social events and these are the people you need to get to know you" (Participant 14a). The participant intoned that those who attend the social events are those who he would rather not interact with.

Participant 10a stated that "attending company activities, golf tournament, and interact with senior management might get them to know you, warm up to you and may help in career progression" (Participant 10a). He continued to say that attending social events may help in getting into the right circles of people and hopefully get a promotion. But he is unable to attend most activities that take place after work hours because he has a young family. He has to rush home after work to pick up the kids. In a resigned tone, the participant said that "it is difficult to compete with people without kids and have time to socialize" (Participant 10a). Similar sentiments were expressed by participant 3a who acknowledged that attending social events is crucial, but she has no time for it because of the family. The participant said that;

Business is done on those social events, help in getting to know new clients, which projects are coming in, and get good assignments. Socializing is important, but I have no time. You have to be engaged, but it is hard. You have to go to those meetings or events and know what is going on. Someone will remember you (Participant 3a).

Participant 11a had different views on why he chooses not to get involved in some social events. The participant posited that growing up in Kenya there are many things anyone can ask anybody and in the U.S. there are things that cannot be asked. The participant admits that his social background is different from the social environment in the U.S. and especially at work. As a result, the people he associates with at work are different from those he associates with outside of work. The participant maintains separate social groups and acts differently in each group. His reasoning was that:

As managers, there are things we are advised not to discuss with employees such as religion, sexual orientation or personal life. We are sensitized to an extent that it limits what we can discuss and hence have less to talk about. This protects me, but it is hard to hold conversations for long (Participant 11a).

Participant 18a indicated that his organization has been experiencing a lot of changes at the executive level. For some reasons, executives are not staying long enough in the organization to establish a concrete relationship. On average executives are staying in the organization for about a year and move on. The participant also said that "every time we have a new executive, there are few new guys coming along and affects what we are doing" (Participant 18a). Participant 20a agrees that allowing executives to bring new people from outside the organization leads to lower morale in the organization and as a result the social aspect is absent. Participant 6a adds that "the social ties or contracts people have from previous organizations allow them to move forward and inhibit others who may be well placed to take those roles" (Participant 6a). The participant believes that lack of social opportunities to be tied with one another outside of work can inhibit growth within the organization.

The social environment can play a significant role in being given a chance to be a leader. Participant 1a, 2a, 4a, 12a, and 16a, believed that understanding the social climate by knowing who to talk to, who to call or lean on, who can promote, and get the training on people skills can be valuable toward attaining leadership position in the organization. Participant 17a argued that more connections and networks happen in social settings, and the absence of that can have an effect.

Theme 3: **Leadership Process**

Interview question 5 probed for views regarding the leadership process in participants' organizations. These entailed on how individuals can move from one level of management to the next and into leadership positions. Thirteen participants (65%) indicated that the leadership process was not clearly defined in their organization. Lack of a structured leadership process was one of the reasons cited why Kenyan immigrants are still not reaching the executive level of leaderships in their organization. Participant 16a had this to say about the leadership process:

It is supposed to be structured or standardized on how to move from one level to the next and what is required such as tests or courses to take to fill certain positions. But the challenge is maneuvering through the networks that are in the organization. Even if you go through the process, the job might be given to someone else because of the connections to the hiring authorities (Participant 16a).

Participant 10a sounded frustrated that the career path is not clearly stated. He said that "there is no leadership process in place in that if you work for a certain number of years you expects to be promoted. It feels like it is unachievable to get to the top level of leadership such as director and above" (Participant 10a). Participant 12a simply stated, "There is no coherent communication from the leadership to indicate the process that should be followed" (Participant 12a). While 14a who works for a non-profit organization was optimistic when he stated that, "it is not very clear at the moment what to do to become a leader" (Participant 14a)

The leadership changes in some organizations were also cited as the reasons the leadership process was not in place or clearly defined. Participant 17a, 1a, 6a, and 18a indicated that their organizations had changed leadership over the last few years and with each new leadership come new vision and new process. "The leadership changes also create an environment where the leadership styles are also changing. It is difficult to know where we are going as an organization and what is going to happen" (Participant 18a). Participant 6a concurred when he said that;

I have seen a lot of changes on the leadership level,

high turnover, new direction, lack of direction and new vision with every turnover. Sometimes we are not what it is expected of us. There is a huge disconnection on the leadership level. Lack of understanding of business needs, team needs and no continues process we can all sign up to (Participant 6a).

Participant 3a indicated that it is hard to become a leader in her organization, and she is not interested in becoming one. Her reasoning is based on the fact that the current leaders have been there forever since the company started. She feels that she does not stand a chance of becoming a leader in this organization. She stated that;

> It is hard to get to be the leader. The current leaders have been there forever since the company started, and I am not interested in becoming a leader. It is difficult seeing how long some other people who have been there longer and still not getting those positions (Participant 3a).

Participant 9a cited a similar situation in his organization. Considering the organization does not have a defined leadership process and has a very low turnover, the wait can be long. The participant says that "for me to move up, my manager has to leave, or the company creates another position" (Participant 9a)

The lack of leadership process appeared to be one of the barriers affecting the Kenyan immigrants the most. The tone of their voices gave an impression that the participants will thrive in organizations that are well structured on how to climb the corporate ladder. Participant 9a and 16a have been in the same organization for over ten years but still stuck in management level. They both have a master's degree, but it does not seem to have had any positive impact in terms of attaining leadership positions. Just as participant 5a said, "it does not matter how long you have been in the organization" (Participant 5a). In essence, these participants are at the mercy of the organization's leadership.

Theme 4: **Culture**

One criterion that was used to select participants for this study is that they had to be Kenyan-born immigrants. All participants who took part in this study completed their high school education in Kenya, and even some completed their university education before migrating. This is an indication all participants were above the age of 18 at the time of migrating to the U.S. This also means that by the time they migrated, the Kenyan culture was long established. Gilmore and Miller (2013) posited that first-generation immigrants moving from one society to another come along with their cultural values to the new country and they may experience difficulty in adapting to the new society especially if the cultural environment was different from their own. The study revealed that participants' culture is a major impediment to attaining leadership positions in their organization.

Interview questions 6 and 7 were used to solicit for views about organizational culture and if it had any effect on participants ability to attain leadership positions in their organizations. Eighteen participants (90%) indicated that culture had an effect on their ability to attain leadership positions. Participant 12a believed that his cultural background might play a role because he perceives issues differently which may not be aligned with what the organizational leadership is looking for. Participant 19a agreed when he said that, "the way we write in Kenya is different, and the leadership style is also different, which all are barriers" (Participant 19a).

Kenyan immigrants come from a culture that is accustomed to being told what to do and not the other way around. Participant 2a indicated that Kenyan immigrants are not vocal enough and come into the U.S. timid. He said that "We are timid in meetings. Speak when spoken to. Not speaking your mind in the U.S. is taken as lacking the knowledge. It takes a while for people to know your potential" (Participant 2a). Participant 3a adds that "I am not aggressive enough. Kenyan immigrants or Africans are not wired to be aggressive" (Participant 3a). Participant 7a argued that as an immigrant it is important to have a balance of learning the culture, being able to fit and establishing a work ethic. Participant 19a said that it is equally important to understand the organization's culture and expectation and make adjustments that may help in attaining leadership positions.

It was interesting to listen to participant 8a, 13a, and 17a on how they are intimidated by the way Americans express themselves during presentations at work. Participant 8a said that;

> The biggest barrier is that people here talk very too fast, they talk a lot and in my culture, I was not trained to talk a lot. Sometimes when you don't talk that much, people tend to think maybe you don't know until you speak. I like to listen more and not just talk (Participant 8a).

Participant 13a who is a senior manager also said that

Americans have a different way of presenting or expressing themselves, and they are loud and confident on how they present ideas. In comparing the Kenyan and American culture the participant said;

> Kenyan culture is between confidence and pride, sometimes Kenyans tend to slow down to speak and give an impression that they don't know, or they have no idea what they are saying, but people don't realize Kenyans may have better ideas than them. An American person uses large terms giving an impression as being informed. Kenyans don't show off, and this can have an impact in getting those leadership positions (Participant 13a).

Participant 17a who is also a senior manager in his organization provided the background of the people he works with as very good presenters who articulate their points very well in meetings. The participant said that as an immigrant, with English as a second language, and an accent, it is challenging and can be intimidating. The participant said that;

> The background of the people I work with is that they are very good presenters and express themselves very well in board meetings and articulate their points when you listen to them. As an immigrant and English as a second language, it can be intimidating and challenging to compete with them. I have a point that I want to make, but I am competing with people who are at a higher level. That has an impact if that is the only thing they are looking for. But the bay area is diverse, and that makes a difference in having a chance to advance (Participant 17a).

Theme 5: **Economic Environment**

The economic environment played a role in preventing Kenyan immigrants from attaining leadership positions. Eleven participants (55%) indicated that the overall economy of the country and more specifically the financial health of the organization could limit leadership opportunities available in the organization. For example, participant 10a stated that "the organization is not spending money on human resources. The workload is growing but there is no hiring of the work-force. The high-level opportunities are not coming up, and it affects the chances of attaining leadership positions" (Participant 10a). To maintain or cut down the cost of operation, organizations put on hold or eliminate promotions and as a result prevent these participants from ascending into leadership positions.

The financial health of an organization is the key to the survival of any organization. Most of the leadership positions are created based on the availability of resources. This sentiment was captured by participant 12a, 14a and 15a and all three works at non-profit organizations. Participant 12a gave a detailed account of the organization's financial health when he said that;

> The economic environment of an organization is the key to the survival of any organization. This is a non-profit organization and there are no enough resources. There are lots of constraints on what we can do, and we are limited to effectively play our role. Most of the leadership positions are created based on the availability of resources. Since the organization serves in a low-income area, there is a lack of resources and as a

170

result, they create minimal leadership positions (Participant 12a).

Participant 14a goes further to say that he is even worried about keeping his current position because the organization is not stable financially. Participant 15a admits that the economic environment does affect the chances of becoming a leader in the organization. As a manager in the same organization for 12 years, she has seen firsthand the many financial challenges the organization has experienced. Sometimes there are no raises, and it is discouraging to become a leader in this organization. In a resigned manner, she is glad to have a job, and she can't leave because of the economy and she has vested interest in the organization. She said;

> The organization is non-profit and we have many challenges with finances sometimes. We have to pay employees, keep our facilities well equipped, take care of the residents and make sure their needs are met at that takes money. Sometimes we spend more money than what we have and it is a big challenge (Participant 15a).

Participant 13a posited that organizational investors such as for-profit organizations have expectations, and they require those expectations to be met. If the company does not meet the expectations of investors, the investors may decide not to invest in the company for it to grow and resort to reducing costs which may result in doing away with some positions. Participant 2a, 4a, and 17a concurred that the financial health of the organization would have an effect when the company is trying to manage cost, and sometimes there are layoffs and organizational restructuring. Participant 2a said that;

The economy impacts investment decisions and strategy of the organization. Strategic initiatives are not done at the moment because of the economic slowdown. The obstacle is not being able to hire regardless of the heavy workload. Delivering the same amount of work but cannot hire. That also means I cannot move up becomes of the economy (Participant 2a).

Participant 3a also agreed that "if the economic environment is bad, no contracts are coming in. The company will not need a lot of people or hire more people. I may not have a job" (Participant 3a). Participant 1a said that "When the economy is doing well, it helps us change, and everybody is getting opportunities" (Participant 1a). Overall, the economy may impact investment decisions and strategy of the organization. That also means the economy may play a role in preventing participants in this study from moving up the organization's ladder and become leaders.

Theme 6: **Organizational Politics**
Questions 9 and 10 explored participants' feelings regarding politics in their organization and if it had any effect on their ability in attaining leadership positions. All participants admitted that politics was prevalent in their organization, and some believed it does play a role in advancing into leadership positions. Eleven participants (55%) indicated politics was present in their organizations, and it does play a role in preventing them from attaining leadership positions. Nine participants admitted there is politics in the organization but believed it did not play any role as a barrier to their growth or were unaware of its effect.

Participant 11a indicated that politics is prevalent in the organization, he hates politics in the organization, and he tries to find a way to stay out of it. He states that he grew up in a culture which advocated for not blowing your own horn. Individuals just needed to work hard, and they are recognized for their efforts. Instead, he said that "people in the U.S. talk about themselves and try to sell themselves, and it is called self-promotion. In Kenya, this is considered as bragging which is not good" (Participant 11a). The soft-spoken participant finds it hard to operate in a politically charged environment.

Some organizations have more politics than others and in some cases, the leaders are part of the politics. Participant 12a opined that politics in the organization is associated with the leadership. Those who are aligned or have something in common with the leaders of the organization are the ones who get promoted or tend to do better. Those who socialize and hang out with leaders are seen as politically connected. The participant is not politically connected to those in leadership and as an immigrant, he believes he does not have anything in common with the leaders, and this hinders his growth in the organization.

Kenyan immigrants seemed to shy away from politics. Their desire is to work hard and to be rewarded for their efforts. Instead, they encounter organizational politics, and they don't know how to play the political game. Participant 4a stated that "politics in the organization can make it hard to climb up the ranks" (Participant 4a). While participant 18a stated that;

> One thing about Kenyan immigrants is that we don't
> know how to play politics. Those who grew up in

America learn the politics of the place and play it
well. Kenyan immigrants have not learned politics.
We tend to thrive in organizations where you are required to prove what you can do to get you rewarded
or promoted (Participant 18a).

Participant 3a shared her past experience with organizational politics with her previous employer. She does not
know how to deal with politics, and she left the organization
because of it. She said that "some people know how to play
the political game and I am not. I left a full time position for
a contract position. There is no politics in my current organization. That is why I like it now" (Participant 3a). Participant 1a and 20a do not appreciate the politics at their place of
work, and they believe this is unnecessary stress, and they
may even forgo to climb up the corporate ladder just to avoid
politics. Participant 20a had this to say about politics;

There is a lot of politics in the organization more than
any other organization I have ever worked for before. I
have worked for two large companies, and I have not
witnessed this kind of politics. I am not a political person, I don't appreciate it, I don't like politics and I stay
away from politics (Participant 20a).

Participant 10a indicated that even though he does not like
playing the political game, he may have to if it means he
would get a promotion. He said that "for me to get a promotion I have to play the politics. You have to be part of those
circles to move up" (Participant 10a). Participant 1a and 17a
agrees with 10a that Kenyan immigrants may have to move
out of their comfort zones in order to attain leadership posi-

tions. Participant 17a reveals that he gets into organizational politics if necessary when he indicated that "I tend not to get in the middle of it because I don't like it but for some people it is a game in corporate America. I avoid it as much as I can and get involved only if I have to" (Participant17a).

Organizational politics can also deny qualified people an opportunity to advance to leadership positions. Participant 6a contended that those in leadership positions decide who should be given an opportunity to advance to join them or not. He gave an example when he said that;

> If your vice president who has been assigned to a role thinks that someone he or she used to work with in a different division is the right person, they are not going to give you an opportunity to make your case. They will push for the person who they think is the right person. They are going to push them through regardless whether they can do the job or not. They will push whoever they want (Participant 6a).

The nature of the workplace has continued to change for the last few years because of the limited job opportunities especially in Northern California. As a result, 14a believes that employees start jostling and undermining each other in order to gain political mileage. He said that "you find that people start backbiting, sabotaging each other, talking who is doing what, who is not doing enough, and a little mistake could become big and cost you a job. It's hard sometimes to play the political game" (Participant 14a). Unfortunately, leaders allow politics to continue unabated, and those who are politically connected become bolder and up their game.

Discrimination

The perception of Kenyan immigrants is that discrimination plays a role in preventing them from attaining leadership positions in their organizations. Even though Northern California is diverse with immigrants from other countries, participants felt that discrimination does not only include the color of their skin but also their national origin. Immigrants from other countries who are the majority tend to stick together and silently give each other opportunities that could otherwise go to those who are qualified. Thirteen participants (65%) believed that since Kenyans are a minority they have to be really good at what they do to be recognized. Participant 19a who has a doctorate on managing school financing chose the field because it is difficult to be discriminated against considering not too many people are involved. "Having the right skills set, experience, and education may make it difficult to be discriminated against" (Participant 19a). But he admits that it was difficult initially to get in when he said that, "first it was not easy going through the door because my last name sometimes betrayed me when I sent out applications" (Participant 19a). If his name were Smith he believed, he would have had it easy to get an interview. He further said that as he continues to grow in his organization, racism becomes a factor because he is considered a minority or the other.

Participant 16a believed that "there are challenges on upward mobility due to biases that exist and there is discrimination that is going on the organization even though it is not official" (Participant 16a). Participant 1a added that "sometimes there is bias on those to promote based on who is making the decisions to promote" (Participant 1a). Even though discrimination is against the law, organizations can practice it through their hiring practices to include or exclude certain races by the number of minorities they hire. The organization of participant 7a appears to fall in this category. Out of 200 hundred employees in his department, there were only three blacks who happened to be African, and since one left the organization, only two are remaining. The participant indicated that, "

> There is a feeling that sometimes we are associated or seen as representatives of African Americans and that it is our role to be seen, not necessarily to contribute to the bottom line of the company and not to be put in sensitive positions of the company (Participant 7a).

Women sometimes are faced with double discrimination based on their race and gender. Participant 20a explained that her organization is family owned, and the origin of the family comes from a community that believes that a woman should be seen and not heard. Her chance of attaining leadership position in this organization is severely limited. Every time there is a promotion it goes to the family's relatives or country men. As someone who comes from a minority race, she believes she has to work ten times harder than everyone else to be acknowledged and this is a challenge. She said that "I am appreciated as a Kenyan immigrant, as a hard worker, appreciated by my deliverables but I do not see that appreciation translating to growth in the organization" (Participant 20a).

Participant 9a had an interesting view regarding discrimination when he said that, "having a mind-set thinking that this is America and people treat me differently because I am a foreigner will definitely affect you" (Participant 9a). He suggested that it is important to perform assigned duties effectively and follow the organization's policy. Soon or later it may become difficult for management to ignore you. His experience included working for the same organization for 15 years, and four years ago he joined the management team. He believes that perseverance pays.

Participant 4a believes that as an immigrant, "you have to prove yourself beyond the other American people who were born here regardless of a college education. With the accent, people will mimic you. You will have closed doors unless you come up and prove yourself" (Participant 4a). Participant 5a is more bothered by employees who ignore his directions and imitate him. Reporting them to upper management will make things worse, and he may have difficulty in managing the employees. The participant appeared frustrated with the group of employees he is managing. He had considered quitting, but he has a family to support.

Four participants indicated that it appears there is a glass ceiling in their organization on how far up in management an immigrant could go. The views of participant 19a were that "experience and education can open doors and as you go higher but there are limitations there" (Participant 19a). While participant 2a suggested that, "at some point there is a ceiling: there are fewer blacks in decision-making positions, and it is difficult to break the ceiling" (Participant 2a). Participant 5a and 7a said that there are opportunities to be promoted into upper management positions, but there is a ceiling how far up one can go. Stereotypes may also play a role in preventing participants from attaining leadership positions.

Participant 14a who is a journalist stated that his abilities and education are sometimes doubted. He said that;

> As a writer, some of my colleagues do not believe I write the reports that I do, and it bothers me. They do not believe I am capable of writing the way I do. The stereotyping can really affect my ability to attain leadership position in the organization (Participant 14a).

Summary

The data collection process for the current study began in March 2016 and lasted until June 2016. The research process involved identifying the study population, obtaining permission to use the non-government organization members and name, and a commitment to purposive sampling method. Other activities included collecting informed consent forms from study participants, scheduling and conducting face-to-face interviews, data collection and analysis and, and finally, the arrangement of data through the themes that emerged. Twenty participants who held mid to senior level management positions participated individually in the semi-structured interview questions. As shown in Figure 4, seven comprehensive themes emerged from the grouping, analysis, and the synthesizing of data generated from participants' lived experience assisted in answering the research question: How do Kenyan immigrants in mid to senior management positions perceive and describe their experiences on barriers in attaining leadership positions? The themes that emerged were: (a) networking, (b) social environment, (c) leadership process, (d) culture, (e) economic environment, (f) organization politics, and (g) discrimination.

Chapter 4 provides a detailed discussion and analysis of

the research results in this qualitative phenomenological study. Some of the discussion included the research question, pilot test, the data collection process, demographic information, data analysis procedure, and the study results. The findings indicated the existence of barriers as described by Kenyan immigrants living through cultural, social, political, and economic barriers in attaining leadership positions in their organizations in Northern California. Chapter 5 provides a brief review of previous Chapters 1, 2, 3, and 4, the study findings, the significance of the findings, limitations of the study, and implications of findings. The chapter also provides a recommendation for future actions and recommendation for future research studies. A summary is provided at the end of the chapter.

Chapter 5
Conclusions and Recommendations

Organizational leaders must be seen to be leading from the front and modeling appropriate behaviors that employees can follow. Platow et al., (2015) observed that leadership is not about individuals who occupy roles but instead it is about group roles. Platow et al., (2015) also noted that there could be no leader without followers.

The current study explored in-depth, the insights and experiences of 20 Kenyan immigrants in mid to senior management positions in various organizations in Northern California regarding the barriers phenomenon. Information shared and results presented in Chapter 4 revealed useful themes that formed the foundation for the study's conclusion. According to Leedy and Ormrod (2010), data interpretation and conclusions drawn in a research endeavor to assign a larger meaning to the data. Chapter 5 concludes the findings underscoring major results bounded by the evidence collected under the following headings: (a) review of previous chapters, (b) findings, (c) significance of the findings, (d) limitations of the study, (e) implications of findings, (f) recommendations for future actions, and (g) recommendations for future research studies.

Review of Previous Chapters

Using a qualitative method and a phenomenological research design, the study explored the lived experiences and perceptions of 20 Kenyan immigrants in mid to senior management positions purposefully selected from a non-profit organization in Northern California. The purpose was to better understand barriers impeding promotion opportunities to leadership positions. The data collection was accomplished through conducting face-to-face, digitally recorded interviews, observations, and review of documents. A modified Van Kaam's seven-step process (Moustakas, 1994) and NVivo 11 computer data analysis software (QSR International, 2016) was used in organizing and analyzing the transcribed data for emergent themes.

In *Chapter 1,* an explanation of the purpose of the current study was provided by describing the background and identified the need for the qualitative study. The general problem explained in the study was barriers immigrants' faced in attaining leadership positions in private and public organizations in the United States. The specific problem was barriers Kenyan immigrants in mid to senior management positions faced in attaining leadership positions in private and public organizations in Northern California. Chapter 1 was also used to explain the significance of the study, the nature of the study, the research question was stated and provided the theoretical framework that would support the research design of the study. The lack of information in the existing studies regarding Kenyan immigrants as leaders or chief executive officers (CEO) in any organization in Northern California was cited as one of the underlying support for pursuing the research study. The definition of terms relevant to migrants and important to the research was provided. Also addressed were assumptions of the study, scope of the study, limitations, and delimitations of the study.

In *Chapter 2,* an extensive review of the literature that evaluated relevant literature that helped to establish a historical perspective of immigrants and migration was provided. The literature included the history of Kenyan immigrants in the U.S., and immigrants' cultural, social, political, and economic barriers perceived to be preventing Kenyan immigrants from advancing into leadership positions in their respective organizations in Northern California. The discussion in this chapter also included leadership theories and models that were relevant to this study, and gaps in the literature were highlighted and used in the final analysis. The gap identified in the literature review was inadequate information on cultural, social, political and economic barriers immigrants in mid to senior management positions faced in advancing to leadership positions in their organizations.

In *Chapter 3*, a detailed explanation of the procedure and

steps taken to obtain and analyze data for this study was provided. The discussion covered areas of qualitative research method and phenomenological research design used to collect data. The discussion included the design appropriateness in relation to the purpose statement, the research question that guided this study, and the demographic information of the population involved in the study. The interview technique was explained along with the analysis of data using a modified Van Kaam method (Moustakas, 1994) as organizing the data, exploring the data, developing themes from the data, reporting the data, interpreting the data, validating the accuracy and credibility of the findings. The chapter also covered information about the sampling procedures, informed consent, confidentiality information, geographic location of the study, the instrument used in the study, data collection strategies, applied data analysis strategies, reliability, and validity.

In *Chapter 4,* a detailed discussion and analysis of the research results in this qualitative phenomenological study was provided. Some of the topics discussed included the research question, pilot test, the data collection process, demographic information, data analysis procedure, and the study results. The chapter provided information about the face-to-face interviews used to conduct the interviews with study participants to gather data and field notes. Data analysis described how the information gathered from the interviews was organized, coded and developed into themes that supported the study. The research study findings described networking, social environment, leadership process, culture, economic environment, organization politics, and discrimination as barriers experienced by the Kenyan immigrants in mid to senior management positions faced in attaining leadership positions in private and public organizations in Northern California.

Findings

The findings identified in this study were significant and supported the existence of the barriers phenomenon. There were two categories of findings that emerged: that supported the existence of barriers (85%), and that did not support the existence of barriers (15%). Seven themes emerged from the coded and counted participants' expressions in Chapter 4. Exploring each theme carefully established the association to the literature reviewed in Chapter 2 and theories framing the study identified in Chapter 1. Interpretation of the study data provided answers to the one central research question guiding the study: How do Kenyan immigrants in mid to senior management positions perceive and describe their experiences on barriers in attaining leadership positions?

Finding 1: Networking

Major findings in the current study included participants' experience of lacking proper networks and mentors to assist in advancing to leadership positions. Networking is a goal-directed behavior that occurs inside and outside of a private or public organization, focused on cultivating, creating, and utilizing relationships between people (Gibson, Hardy, & Buckley, 2014; McCallum, Forret, & Wolff, 2014). The purpose of networking is to develop deeper relationships with those in influential positions in an organization with the intent of increasing visibility, access to strategic information and career success (Gibson et al., 2014). As participant 1a noted "you have to know people and they have to know you. Otherwise it is hard to sell yourself. You must know who is up there, who is going to promote you. Work with them to know they can depend on you, they know you and when promotion comes you have a chance" (Participant 1a). Networking can facilitate the development of personal and professional opportunities and can be valuable for ambitious individuals.

The discoveries in the current study are similar to the existing literature review findings of Gibson et al. (2014) and Butler (2008) that emphasized the need for understanding the role of networking inside and outside organizations. Gibson et al. (2014) posited that networking can facilitate the development of personal and professional opportunities, contribute to the functioning of the organization, improve communication, and access to resources. Gibson et al. (2014) suggested that the quality of one's network carries as great or greater of an influence on an individual's career success than their abilities, knowledge, and experience, a belief summarized by the common maxim, "it's not what you know, it's who you know" (p. 146). Similar views were expressed by participant 8a and 16a. Participant 8a said that "the more people you know, the better network you have the better the chances" (Participant 8a). While participant 16a noted that "it depends on who you know and how much effort you put into it" (Participant 16a). As a result, networking is held to be of great professional value for ambitious individuals and organizations, and it is important for individuals to develop and nurture their networks that can help in career progression.

Butler (2008) emphasized that networking is rapidly being recognized as a critical business, career and leadership skill. Networking is building and maintaining helpful connections and relationships with other people for mutual benefit (Mc-

Callum, Forret, & Wolff, 2014). Those who are network building savvy within organizations will reap the rewards of rapid career progression, leadership opportunities, greater job satisfaction and business success (Butler, 2008). To be successful, individuals need to understand the role of networking and apply it in order to maximize the opportunities networking can provide. Failure to build useful networks within the organization will result in slow career progression or career stagnation.

Mentoring is also closely related to networking. Mentoring involves an experienced person providing guidance, counseling, assistance or helping a younger or new employees to develop leadership skills in order to advance or succeed in the organization (Corner, 2014; Dunbar, & Kinnersley, 2011; Lanna-Lipton, 2007). The relationship between the mentor and mentee benefits both parties. The mentee benefits by learning the much-needed leadership skills and gains experience that he or she needs to succeed in the organization. Whereas, the mentor gains the satisfaction of passing on the experience, wisdom, and developing the new talent. As expressed by participant 10a in regard to the Kenyan immigrants, he said that "we lack mentors who can guide others and we are as a result disadvantaged working in the U.S. especially in information technology field" (Participant 10a).

Finding 2: Social Environment

The study findings supported the research that immigrants are faced with many social challenges that affect their growth in organizations (Jimenez, 2011). Each participant expressed concerns about their inability to attend social events at their

work place, and balancing work and family was an impediment to their growth in the organization. Hurtado-de-mendoza, et al., (2014) argued that as social beings, people
require social networks that provide social support, influence,
engagement and interpersonal contact for their wellbeing. As
participant 17a indicated "more connections and networks
happen in social settings and if you don't have them, it can
have an effect" (Participant 17a). Another participant, 4a,
also said that "the social environment can play a significant
role in being given a chance to be a leader" (Participant 4a).
The participants' experience support the idea that a lack of social support in the organization may lead to social isolation
(Shinnar, 2007), which may have a negative impact on immigrants' advancing to leadership positions.

The Kenyan immigrants testified that their inability to attend organizational events outside work hours to interact with
senior management due to work-family conflict may have
limited their chances of advancing to leadership positions.
Consistent with Rathi and Barath, (2013), the time required
by managerial work and that of family care is one of the
major challenges experienced by individuals with families.
To collaborate with this finding, participant 10a stated "I have
a young family and I may not go to golf tournaments to socialize or to network after work or during weekends and that
can put me at a disadvantage or affect my chances" (Participant 10a). Participant 13a and 8a experienced a similar situation as participant 10a. Participant 13a believed that
socializing with co-workers in and outside the company is a
good way to know other people and may help in growing in
the organization. But he said "sometimes I may not attend
some of these events because I have a family and I have to go

home immediately after work" (Participant 13a). While participant 3a said "I have no time to attend social events because of work and family balancing" (Participant 3a).

Seventy percent of the participants acknowledged struggling to strike a balance between work and family. Most challenges shared comprised of participation in the work role was made more difficult by the virtue of participation in the family role (Baral, & Bhargava, 2010; Burgess, & Waterhouse, 2010; Odle-dusseau, Britt, & Bobko, 2012; Rathi & Barath, 2013). Participant 8a shared that she was struggling with balancing her job and the family. She said that "sometimes my colleagues want to go out for lunch or dinner but I can't since I am thinking of going to pick up my kids from school" (Participant 8a). Given her situation, the participant has to pick her family over her social life with co-workers. It was difficult for participants especially those with young children to attend social events after work hours or outside the organization. Fourteen participants (70) agreed that it is difficult to compete for leadership positions with those who have grown children or have no children.

Finding 3: Leadership Process

The third theme that developed from these data was a lack of a defined leadership process that participants can subscribe to in their organizations. The challenges were described as a lack of a structured leadership process, lack of communication from leadership on the direction of the organization, and unpredictable organizational changes. The lack of specific or standardized information on what it takes to move up the corporate ladder was discussed under this theme as the Kenyan immigrants spoke of lack of leadership development, management, role models, and training of employees.

The current study findings emphasized the important role that leaders play in shaping the culture of the organization through their behaviors (Kouzes & Posner, 2003). Kouzes and Posner, (2003) found that leaders modeling appropriate behaviors are effective, and their behaviors help employees to improve the work environment. Kouzes and Posner (2003) concluded that five exemplary leadership behaviors are essential for novice leaders in any private or public organization. The five leadership behaviors included modeling the way, inspiring a shared vision, challenging the process, enabling others to act, and encouraging the heart (Boyd, 2014; Hutton, 2012; Kouzes & Posner, 2002). The study findings revealed that the Kenyan immigrants wanted to model appropriate behaviors that benefited their organizations but it was either lacking or haphazard. The Kenyan immigrants were left with the responsibility to model appropriate behavior in their organizations.

Thirteen participants in the current study expressed concerns about the lack of a structured leadership process to follow in attaining leadership positions. As a result some participants were discouraged from pursuing career development in their organizations and become leaders. Participants' phrases and sentences were dominated by words such as limited, not interested, unachievable, unpredictable, disconnected, ineffective, rigid and undefined. These findings therefore revealed a leadership process that was haphazard and could be manipulated. The findings revealed organizational changes were partly to blame for the undefined leadership process. As participant 18a noted "the leadership changes also create an environment where the leadership styles are also changing. It is difficult to know where we are going and what is going to happen" (Participant 18a). Participant 17a also stated that "the organization has changed leadership over the last few years and with each new leadership comes new vision and new process" (Participant 17a). Due to lack of organization and coordination, haphazard communication, and unpredictable organizational environment, the findings showed that participants were not motivated to seek leadership positions in various organizations. Yukl (2013) posited that it is the responsibility of leaders to act to improve subordinates' motivation. Yukl (2013) goes on to state that "leaders can motivate subordinates by influencing their perceptions about the likely consequences of different levels of effort" (p. 164). As expressed by participant 15a that "if I am offered a position and I am not comfortable taking it I will decline it and request to be placed where I will excel" (Participant 15a). Subordinates performance would be improved when they have clear and accurate role expectations, the task objectives are achievable, the necessary training was provided, and the perception that high performance will result in beneficial outcomes. Nahavandi (2012) noted that the key to motivation is for leaders to remove any obstacles that weaken the linkages between effort and performance and between performance and outcomes. The study results indicated the Kenyan immigrants were faced with obstacles that led to a lack of motivation. Removal of various obstacles would motivate them to seek leadership positions.

Finding 4: Culture

The current literature review findings revealed that cultural barriers play a role in leadership across cultural boundaries.

The study findings were consistent with the current literature findings of Dickson et al., (2012) and Dorfman et al., (2012) who found that there are cultural variations in leadership, and there are aspects of leadership characteristics that are universal, and that pertains to specific cultures. The universal leadership characteristics are generally accepted across cultures, whereas the cultural leadership characteristics are accepted in specific societies. Gilmore and Miller (2013) found that immigrants who moved from one society to another experienced difficulty in adapting to the new society especially when there are significant cultural differences. As participant 12a noted, "my cultural background may also play a role because I perceive things differently which may not be aligned with what the organizational leadership is looking for" (Participant 12a). Participant 19a supports participant 12a views when he said that "even the way we write in Kenya is different and the leadership style is also different, which all are barriers" (Participant 19a). Another participant said that "differences in culture are the biggest barriers. In Californian and specifically in Silicon Valley there are diverse cultures and you have to adapt and learn how organizations work" (Participant 13a). Adapting to a new culture is never easy but it is necessary to achieve leadership positions in a society with diverse cultural backgrounds.

The Kenyan culture is significantly different from the United States culture, and the findings revealed cultural variations hinders the career growth of Kenyan immigrants in the United States. Dickson et al. (2012) concluded that culture does matter in how leaders become visible, are selected, are developed, and recognized or not recognized as role models to be emulated. Culture matters in ways that can be predicted, and in ways organizations can respond to strategically. As participant 2a stated "as an immigrant you need to have a balance of learning the culture, being able to fit, establishing work ethic and looking at the big picture" (Participant 2a).

The culture was one of the most widespread themes in the data. A study conducted by Hofstede suggested that there are five dimensions of national culture describing routines, norms and attitudes of people (The Hofstede Centre, 2015). The five cultural dimensions included power distance, uncertainty avoidance, individualism, masculinity, and long-term orientation (Shah et al., 2011; The Hofstede Centre, 2015). The study findings revealed how different countries deals with social inequality, the relationship that exists between the individual and the group, expresses the dominant values in the society, copes with uncertainty, and different ways of dealing with or handling the present and the future. Culture does have an effect on leadership effectiveness in different regions differently (Shah et al., 2011).

The Kenyan immigrants also highlighted the importance of communication across cultures because it plays a role in leadership determination process. The research findings on cross-cultural communication by Giri (2006) and Leonard et al., (2009) found that culture and communication are directly linked and have a great influence on each other. Cultural differences can sometimes make communication process complicated because of the variations in interpersonal interactions (Giri, 2006). Participant 2a had this to say about Kenyan immigrants' culture, "we are timid in meetings. Speak when spoken to. Not speaking your mind in U.S. is taken as lacking the knowledge. It takes a while for people to know your potential" (Participant 2a). Sometimes by the time organization realize the potential of immigrants it is too late, and someone else has been offered the leadership opportunity. Participant 2a acknowledges the fact that nothing comes easy to anybody and a result, Kenya immigrants need to raise up their hands, speak up to move up the ranks, and obtain leadership positions.

The literature revealed that communication style of Kenyan immigrants is different from that of the Americans (Shah et al., 2011), and may play a role in determining their growth in the organization. A significant number perceived career advancement for American colleagues as smooth and fast. The Kenyan immigrants perceive issues differently, write differently, speak differently and lead differently, which puts them at a disadvantage. The literature further indicated that Kenyan immigrants are not aggressive enough to know what they want and go for it, and they speak when spoken to, creating an impression of lacking in leadership abilities.

Finding 5: Economic Environment

The unfavorable economic environment and more specifically the financial health of organizations were cited as one of the barriers that played a role in holding back the Kenyan immigrants from advancing to leadership positions. The findings revealed that the financial health of organizations determines the creation or elimination of leadership opportunities. Lack of resources forces organizations to put on hold or eliminate management promotions.

In collaboration with this finding, participant 12a stated that "most of the leadership positions are created based on the availability of resources. Since the organization serves in a low-income area, there is a lack of resources and as a result, they create minimal leadership positions" (Participant12a). The same views were expressed by participant 10a when he said "the organization is not spending money on human resources. The workload is growing but there is no hiring of the workforce. The high-level opportunities are not coming up and it affects the chances of attaining leadership positions" (Participant 10a. As a result, the Kenyan immigrants are either stuck in the same positions or are prevented from ascending to leadership positions.

The study findings supported research that immigrants come to the United States in search of economic opportunities. For that reason, immigrants are more than willing to take any jobs when they first arrive in the U.S. due to their poor economic background and in the long run, this fact denies them valuable experience and opportunities (Shinnar, 2007). Immigrants may also be passed over for promotion opportunities because of lack of experience in their area of expertise (Shinnar, 2007). The skilled, educated and talented immigrants coming to the U.S. also have difficulty in finding jobs and promotions because their education and skills may not be recognized by American organizations (Borah, 2013; Shinnar, 2007; Tyler & Petsod, 2003). Some immigrants with Kenyan degrees expressed that their skills and education were questioned by various organizations. As participant 18a said;

> Coming with a degree from Kenya people are suspicious and are not sure what you did. What do they teach you in Africa, they ask? They don't know how much you know, you have to prove what you know. Having to prove myself because of the foreign education is always taxing (Participant 18a).

Participant 13a who received a bachelor's degree in Kenya had a similar experience as 18a, and he indicated that some people did not understand the quality of Kenya's education. The participant said that "people not understanding the degree coming from Kenya is worth the paper it is written on is frustrating. You have to prove yourself that the work you do is in a standard that is acceptable" (Participant 13a). Because of these facts, and the unfavorable financial health of organizations, the Kenyan immigrants are competitively disadvantaged. In essence, unfavorable economic environment affected the Kenyan immigrants' career development in their organizations.

Finding 6: Organizational Politics

Congruent with current study findings, eleven Kenyan immigrants experienced stifling organization politics and recognized it as a barrier to the effective performance of employees in an organization. The majority of Kenyan immigrants acknowledged the existence of organization politics and its role in denying them the opportunity to advance to leadership positions considering they are not good at it. The current research study findings are similar to the existing literature review findings by Ramírez Solís, Monroy, and Orozco-Gómez (2014) that viewed organizational politics as a barrier to the effective performance of employees within a firm. Bukhari and Kamal (2015) found that the goal of individuals involved in organizational politics is furthering one's own self-interests without regard for the well-being of others or that of their organization. Gotsis and Kortezi (2011) indicated that organization politics consists of intentional acts of influence or use and exercise of power to gain access to scarce resources, and the use of actions and tactics aiming to influence decision making.

Gotsis and Kortezi, (2011) noted that some of the organizational politics involves anti-social behaviors such as, "blaming, manipulating and attacking others, by-passing proper superiors, withholding information, ingratiating and praising others, creating and maintaining a favorable image through impression management, developing coalitions with powerful and influential persons" (p. 451). In collaboration with the findings, participant 14a believes that organizational politic is not good for business, and it is fueled by the limited job opportunities. The participant said that;

The nature of workplace has continued to change for the last few years. Because of the limited job opportunities, you find that people start backbiting, sabotaging each other, talking who is doing what, who is not doing enough, and a little mistake could become big and cost you a job" (Participant 14a).

Gotsis and Kortezi, (2011) found that organizational politics was an informal, non-sanctioned behavior that may be detrimental to achieving organizational goals. Organizational politics is contrived to benefit an individual or specific groups of people using various means to achieve preferred outcomes.

The findings by Ramírez Solís et al., (2014) suggested that there is evidence in the respective literature that indicates the negative effects of political behavior on the job. The negative perceptions of organizational politics are associated with employees having lower job satisfaction, lower organizational commitment, lower organizational citizenship behavior, and overall organizational performance. The perception of organizational politics is harmful to organizational life because it leads to job anxiety, stress, withdrawal behaviors, and intentions to leave the organization (Ramírez Solís, et al., 2014). As expressed by participant 3a, she left an organization because the politics was too much to bear. She said that "I left my previous organization because of the politics. I left a full time position for a contract position" (Participant 3a). Organizational politics change the climate in an organization and as a result, Kenyan immigrants either leave or shy from seeking leadership positions because they don't like to be involved, and they don't know how to play politics.

Finding 7: Discrimination

The final theme that developed from these data was the perceived racial discrimination biases toward the Kenyan immigrants. The barriers ware described as challenges on upward mobility due to biases that exist, which includes racial and national origin discrimination that goes on in organizations. The findings in the literature indicated that discrimination and prejudice are still prevalent in the American society (Lucas, et al., 2014). The Kenyan immigrants are assimilated into the American society as blacks or African Americans, and their lives are shaped by the existing racial classifications (Wamwara-Mbugua, et al., 2006). Kenyan immigrants indicated that they are not only dealing with racial bias (Lucas, et al., 2014) but also their national origin because of the accent that gives them away (Wamwara-Mbugua & Cornwell, 2010). Being an African and an immigrant is a double-edged sword, and it is a challenge in attaining leadership positions.

Eight participants in this study revealed that they had experienced racial discrimination and biases in attaining leadership positions in their organizations. For example, participant 19a indicated that as an African and immigrant it is not easy to become a leader in the United States because of discrimination and racial bias. The participant said it is a challenge to even get an interview because of his African name. He said that "it was not easy going through the door because my last name sometimes betrays me when I send out applications" (Participant 19a). The participant believed that having a name such as Smith would have at least allowed him to obtain an interview. The participant continued to say that as a site manager he still experiences biases when he said that "in growing in the organization you are still the other. When moving higher up, racism becomes a factor" (Participant 19a).

Participant 4a and 1a experience collaborated with the participant 19a's experience. Participant 4a stated that "as an immigrant, you have to prove yourself beyond the other American people who were born here regardless of college education. With the accent people will mimic you. You will have closed doors unless you come up and prove yourself" (Participant 4a). While participant 1a stated that "sometimes there is bias on those to promote based on who is making the decisions to promote" (Participant 1a).

All participants in this study acknowledged that for Kenyan immigrants to attain leadership positions, they must excel at what they do and work hard to be promoted into leadership positions. Even then, there is a ceiling on how far up the Kenyan immigrants could go because of discrimination. As expressed by participant 2a, 5a, 7a and 19a, there are fewer black people in decision making positions in their organizations and there is a ceiling how far up in management they could go and it is difficult to break it.

Significance of the Findings

The findings in this study support those of previous studies found in the current literature review for this research. Findings developed by the current research study confirmed and supported prior literature on cultural, social, political, and economic barriers were hindering career development for immigrants in the United States (Kameny et al. 2014; Shinnar, 2007; Takougang & Tidjani, 2009; Yakushko et al., 2008). The findings indicated that these barriers continue to negatively affect immigrants' productivity, raising the concerns regarding the effectiveness of the many discrimination laws and policies in the United States (De George, 2010). Leaders may use the findings as an environment scanning tool to identify the cultural, social, political, and economic barriers working against immigrants in their organizations.

Organizational barriers can become costly in terms of turnover costs, as affected qualified immigrants leave the organization (Shinnar, 2007; Yukl, 2013). The results of this study revealed crucial factors that limited the career development of the Kenyan immigrants even after rising up to the management levels. Organizational leaders and policy makers may use the study results to develop policies that encourage and recognize the contribution of immigrants to achieve organizational goals, and give them opportunities to advance to leadership positions. Nahavandi (2012) emphasized the need for organizations to change how they manage and train employees, and rewrite their policies to address the needs of diverse communities. The study's discoveries may compel organizational leaders to compare their performance and corporate governance with other organizations whose structure embraces diversity in strategic decision-making positions.

Limitations of the Study

The purpose of this qualitative phenomenological research study was to explore the lived experiences and perceptions of Kenyan immigrants in mid to senior management positions to better understand barriers impeding promotion opportunities to leadership positions in Northern California. In research studies, limitations are used to detect potential study weaknesses (Leedy & Ormrod, 2010; Simon, 2006). Neuman (2009) referred to limitations as threats to the internal validity that may reflect or reveal weaknesses in a given study. The major limitation encountered in the current study included the threat of inadequate data often prompted by the honesty of participants. The study relied on participants' honesty, a virtue that is subjective and cannot be fully guaranteed.

Another limitation was that in some situations, participants' ethnicity, gender, or social status may have influenced their answers (Leedy, & Ormrod, 2010). Another limitation to this study was the nature of the sample itself. Although the sample size is good (n=20), there were disproportionate numbers of men and women (16 and 4, respectively). In a few instances, some participants allocated inadequate time for the interviews hindering full exploitation of experiences. The unique experiences of the 20 participants might not represent all methods available to senior managers in private or public organization in Northern California to overcome the barriers in attaining leadership positions. Another limitation was that the study limited its sample collection from the Kenyan community's non-profit organization located in Northern California. The results might have been different if the study considered the lived experiences of Kenyan immigrants living in each of the 49 states in the U.S.

Implications of Findings

The implication of the findings from the current study was that the seven themes that emerged from the participants' responses resonated with all the participants as far as the barriers in attaining leadership positions in their organizations were concerned. Each participant's response presented their view about the barriers encountered played a role in preventing them from advancing to leadership positions. The seven themes that resulted from the study's findings included networking, social environment, leadership process, culture, economic environment, organization politics, and discrimination. The first theme was related to creating proper networks within the organization that may be utilized for career advancements. Evidence presented by Gibson et al. (2014) indicated that developing a deeper working relationship with those in leadership positions would increase one's visibility, access to strategic information and may translate to career success.

The second theme addressed findings associated with participants' inability to attend workplace social events, and challenges balancing work and family was an impediment to their growth in the organization. The studies by Hurtado-demendoza et al., (2014) found that as social beings, it is important for people to establish social networks that provide social support, influence, engagement and interpersonal contact for their wellbeing. The third theme was associated with lack of a structured leadership development process, communication, and organizational changes. Leaders play an important role in shaping the culture of the organization through their behaviors. Applying the five exemplary leadership behaviors as discussed by Kouzes and Posner (2003) remain an attractive option.

The fourth theme focused on cultural variations in leadership and its role across cultural boundaries. Understanding and adapting leadership characteristics that are acceptable across cultures will lead to leadership effectiveness in different societies (Dickson et al., 2012; Shah et al., 2011), and beneficial to career development. The fifth theme dealt with the unfavorable economic environment and its effect on career development. Experience and acquiring relevant skills and education may facilitate promotional opportunities (Shinnar, 2007. The sixth theme addressed the effects of politics in organizations. The study findings by Gotsis and Kortezi (2011) indicated that organizational politics is detrimental to achieving organizational goals because of its self-serving behaviors that disregard the well-being of others and the organization. The evidence suggests that organizational policies that treat everyone equally would be perceived as supportive. The final and seventh theme addressed the issue of perceived racial discrimination and biases. Studies by Lucas et al., (2014) noted the prevalence of discrimination and prejudice in the American society. Embracing and nurturing diversity in private and public organizations would give everyone equal opportunities to succeed regardless of their race or cultural background.

The aim of the current study was to answer the research question: How do Kenyan immigrants in mid to senior management positions perceive and describe their experiences on barriers in attaining leadership positions? The research question was adequately answered as the data from all the study participants showed the true reflections of Kenyan immigrants' experiences under the phenomenon. Participants' experiences were organized into seven relevant themes namely; networking, social environment, leadership process, culture, economic environment, organization politics, and discrimination. These themes supported the study findings and recommendations. Recommendations of the study discussed in the next section offered effective organizational leadership behaviors and practices to improve the chances of the Kenya immigrants' career advancement endeavors.

Recommendations for Future Actions

Neuman (2009) posited that the benefits of conducting research studies as helping individuals to make more informed decisions, to improve working environments, and an opportunity to acquire new knowledge. The result of the current research findings and conclusions offered an opportunity to provide recommendations for future leaders and future studies in management and organizational leadership. The current study was about identifying the cultural, social, political, and economic barriers impeding promotion opportunities to leadership positions for Kenyan immigrants in mid to senior level management positions in Northern California. To overcome these barriers require effective leaders equipped with transformational competencies to know the steps to take and the pitfalls to avoid preparing for advancing to top leadership positions (Rumano, 2009; Wamwara-Mbugua, Cornwell, & Boller, 2006; Wamwara-Mbugua & Cornwell, 2010).

The recommendations for the Kenyan immigrants were

based on the themes and concepts that were identified in this study. The themes identified in the data analysis described perceived barriers preventing the Kenyan immigrants in advancing to leadership positions in their organizations. The themes that developed from the data may help the immigrants to establish proper networks and mentors to assist in advancing to leadership positions. Practices that encourage being part of the organization's social environment may help in understanding and appreciating individuals from diverse cultural backgrounds. Addressing challenges in the organization's leadership process, culture, politics, and policies may help to improve the work environment, and encourage the Kenyan immigrants to pursue and attain leadership positions. The recommendations are categorized as social networking, developing leadership model, leadership styles, organizational change, and managing diversity.

Social Networking. The first recommendation was the need for Kenyan immigrants in mid to senior level management positions to learn to become effective in social networking and finding mentors inside and outside of their organizations. Evidence from the study results considerably pointed to a lack of social networking and mentoring as contributors to Kenyan immigrant's slow career advancement. Gibson et al., (2014) noted that networking creates, cultivates, and utilizes interpersonal relationships with those in influential positions in an organization with the aim of increasing one's visibility, access to strategic information and career success. Establishing proper social networks in an organization can facilitate developing personal and professional opportunities and can be valuable toward career growth (Gibson et al., 2014). Knowing the right people within an organization and establishing a relationship with those individuals can become valuable when seeking for promotional opportunities. In essence, knowing and being known by those who have the ability to promote is an asset that can be useful when promotions become available.

Gibson et al. (2014) noted that there are a significant number of services available to help individuals to develop and nurture their networks. For example, a variety of books and websites on networking offer readers how to grow and use their networks to achieve success are available. The Kenyan immigrants could also attend professional networking conference sessions to learn how to interact with other people and access websites that provide a technological interface through which individuals can grow and develop their networks (Gibson et al., 2014). Websites such as LinkedIn, BranchOut, or Zerply are designed to help individuals to network and get ahead (Gibson et al., 2014). It is recommended that Kenyan immigrants seek for these services to learn networking concepts that could boost their career growth. It is important for the Kenyan immigrants to create and nurture working relationships with those in leadership positions and those who might come through in a time of need. Butler (2008) noted that those who build quality networks experience rapid career growth, leadership opportunities, greater job satisfaction, and business success.

Finding a mentor who is in a leadership position within the same organization can also play a role in career progression. Experienced mentors provide counsel, guidance, and assistance to employees who are new to the organization to develop needed leadership skills and to advance in the organization (Corner, 2014). Mentors have to be willing, ready, and able to impart organizational knowledge to those mentees who are able and willing to learn. Finding a mentor who is willing and able to guide the Kenyan immigrants may help them to grow in their organizations.

Develop Leadership Model. The second recommendation was for the organizations to develop structured leadership processes or model that can be followed in advancing to leadership positions. Nahavandi (2012) defined development as an ongoing, dynamic, long-term change or evolution that occurs because of various learning experiences. Conner (2000) noted that the process of developing future leaders is complex and organizations need a more structured approach. Companies need to develop a systematic way of identifying potential managers, proactively planning career development, and continuously evaluating the effectiveness of leadership development process (Muchiri & Kiambati, 2015; Platow, Haslam, Reicher, & Steffens 2015; Woodward, More, & Van der Heyden, 2016). The study by Nahavandi (2012) posited that leader development is "expansion of a person's capacity to be effective in leadership roles and processes" (p.309). The focus of leader development is on the individual and involves providing leaders with the tools they need to improve their effectiveness in the various roles they play within the organization (Nahavandi, 2012).

Organizational leaders must be seen to be leading from the front and modeling appropriate behaviors that employees can follow. Platow et al., (2015) observed that leadership is not about individuals who occupy roles but instead it is about group roles. Platow et al., (2015) also noted that there could be no leader without followers. The observation was affirmed by King (2010) who noted that "when individuals follow another's actions, they make that individual a leader" (p.671). A study by Wren (1995) ascribed leadership to the constant interaction of leaders and followers, which is an indication that leaders need followers as much as followers need leaders. The relationship is strengthened where leaders develop followers to become the leaders of the future.

It is also essential that organizational leaders adopt the five exemplary leadership practices as described by Kouzes and Posner (2003) to transform the leadership process in their organizations. Modeling the way, inspiring a shared vision, challenging the process, enabling others to act, and encouraging the heart (Kouzes & Posner, 2003), will not only make leaders effective but also develop and encourage others to become leaders of tomorrow. It is important that leaders model behaviors expected of others, share their vision, take chances on others, involve and strengthen others, and recognize other people's contributions.

Leadership Styles. The third recommendation was for the Kenyan immigrants to learn and adapt leadership styles that are universally acceptable across cultures. Despite the fact that all Kenyan immigrants in this study have been in the United States for more than six years (see Table 2), still, culture plays a role in hindering their career growth. The literature findings indicated that it is important to understand the national culture as to which kinds of leadership would most likely be effective (Dorfman et al., 2012) and adopt it to achieve career development.

For the Kenyan immigrants to succeed in seeking and attaining leadership positions in the U.S., it is important that they adopt leadership styles or behaviors that are acceptable within the American culture. Bass (1997) suggested that transformational leadership appears to be preferred, universally acceptable and effective across cultures. Nahavandi (2012) and Wan Khairuzzaman et al., (2011) also suggested that a combination of transformational and transactional leadership styles may be effective if applied appropriately. It is recommended that Kenyan immigrants learn, adopt and practice transformational leadership concepts, transactional leadership concepts, and as well as LPI model concepts to have a chance or position themselves in advancing to leadership positions. Failure to adopt acceptable leadership styles and behaviors that are acceptable across cultures in the U.S., will confine Kenyan immigrants to managerial positions and hinder their growth.

Nahavandi (2012) contended that a leader is someone who influences individuals and groups in an organization to establish goals, guides them to achieve those goals, and as a result they become effective. Leaders help organizations create order, maintain internal health and external adaptability (Nahavandi, 2012). Leaders also play a special role in creating organizational culture by their decision-making process, reward systems, hiring practices and being role models. Leadership is dynamic and requires flexibility and adaptability to changing global environment. The success of Kenyan immigrants in ascending to leadership positions in the U.S. is pegged on their ability to be flexible and adapting to changing leadership styles in response to global expectations.

Organizational Change. The fourth recommendation was for organizations to create a work environment in which policies and practices are carried out fairly, and the same rules apply equally to everyone. Ramírez Solís et al., (2014) posited that when employees have the confidence and support of their immediate superior, the amount of responsibility and expectations are clearly defined, performance standards are understood and communicated, they are treated as valuable team players, the significance of employee's contribution is recognized, and expression of own feelings encouraged, would create a non-political work climate and organizations would likely not be perceived as political. A non-political work environment would be perceived as a safe and stable environment and as a result will have committed employees to the organization and satisfied with their work (Ramírez Solís et al., 2014). Bukhari and Kamal (2015) concluded that organizations are perceived to be supportive when their policies and practices such as pay, recognition and promotions are perceived to be fair.

It is no secret that leaders play a significant role in making organizational changes and determining the course of the organization in an effort to achieve desired goals. For any meaningful change to take place, it must be supported by the leaders. Yukl (2013) indicated that for organizations to successfully compete in the global environment, they must have leaders who are flexible and willing to change their assumptions and beliefs. Yukl (2013) stated that "One of the most important competencies for successful leadership in changing situations is the ability to learn from experience and adapt to change" (p. 153). As a result, it is recommended that leaders find ways to improve their policies and practices and ensure that they are carried out fairly and adhered to by everyone in the organization.

Managing Diversity. The last recommendation was for organizations to review their policies on diversity, embrace and nurture diversity. Considering Northern California has a diverse population from various cultural backgrounds, immigrants make a significant contribution to the growth of U.S. economy (Davies, 2009). It is imperative that leaders in private and public organizations be more receptive, open, and tolerant of diversity in their organizations (De George, 2010; Nahavandi, 2012; Yukl, 2013). Leaders need to ensure immigrants from different cultural backgrounds are given equal promotion opportunities to lead and not individuals from a few selected nationalities.

The study by Clarke (2005) indicated that work place discrimination and job-related biases are experienced more often by African Americans and women. Studies show that even though organizations actively promote diversity, African Americans and women have or knew someone who had experienced racial or gender discrimination (Hirsh & Lyons, 2010). Despite the fact that organizations have workplace multicultural initiatives, still, some have failed to effectively implement and manage diversity (Clarke, 2005). The failure of diversity was attributed to lack of support from organizational leaders, lack of a clearly defined business case for diversity in the organizations, and general intolerance of differences. Organizational leaders must be involved in building diversity into the organization's foundation for it to succeed by appreciating and valuing the unique differences, contributions, perspectives and experiences (Clarke, 2005; De

George, 2010).

Organizational leaders must create a culture where everyone is tolerated and given an opportunity to succeed (Yukl, 2013). Developing and implementing diversity policies will ensure everyone who qualifies regardless of their cultural background or national origin is given a fair chance to succeed. The study by De George (2010) noted that if organizations did not discriminate, "but hired and promoted only on the basis of merit, they would undoubtedly hire and promote some of those they discriminate against" (p. 357). As a result, organizations are not getting the best people but suffer some harm and experience no benefit. Changes in the social structures of organizations are essential to accommodating individuals from diverse cultural backgrounds.

To effectively manage and achieve diversity, it is recommended that leaders continuously seek a diverse employment environment and support diversity as a goal. Without continuous leadership support, diversity will not be fully achieved. Studies by De George, (2010); Nahavandi (2012); and Yukl (2013) suggested that to achieve diversity, organizational leaders may need to strengthen and improve on diversity awareness and initiatives through deliberate efforts such as;

1. ***Corporate Diversity:*** Organizations are committed to diversity through corporate initiatives.

2. ***Leadership Diversity:*** Ensuring the organization's leadership reflects gender, age, race, and national origin to name a few.

3. ***Cross-Cultural Diversity:*** Leaders encouraging and promoting issues of cross-cultural diversity to create a rapport among cultures in the organization.

4. ***Gender Diversity:*** Organizations promoting gender

diversity with gender equality, education, and leadership development.

Recommendations for Future Research Studies

The current study explored the cultural, social, political, and economic barriers perceived to be preventing Kenyan immigrants in mid to senior management positions from attaining leadership positions in Northern California. Future research to validate the results through a reproduction of this study is recommended. Future researchers can replicate this study by using a qualitative phenomenological study to explore the experiences of immigrants in other states living through similar challenges. One future study could explore barriers immigrants from other countries are faced with in attaining promotion opportunities to leadership positions in another state or regions of the United States. Other research opportunities could be explored using a different theoretical framework to have a different perspective, or to better understand the phenomenon of barriers that prevent immigrants in private or public organizations from advancing to leadership positions. Conducting a study in another geographical location may offer a new set of demographics and resources to carry out the study. Conducting future research study may help identify new information pertaining to cultural, social, political, and economic barriers immigrants encounter in advancing to leadership positions in private or public organizations in the United States.

The limitations of this study were the location of the study, the time available to carry out the study, and the perception of the phenomenon by the study participants and the ability to answer research questions honestly for the focus of the study. Generalizability of the study may be established if additional research studies are conducted in other locations throughout the United States.

While the scope of this research study was specifically limited to first generation Kenyan immigrants in mid to senior level management positions, the data gathered implied a number of factors that may lead to future studies. For instance, as stated in the problem statement, when immigrants arrive in the United States, they are faced with some natural barriers to full social, economic, and political participation (Jimenez, 2011). Over time, the gap narrows as immigrants begin to integrate into the U.S. society, and full integration is achieved in subsequent generations (Gilmore & Miller, 2013). Future qualitative studies may be conducted on second or third generations of Kenyan immigrants' regarding barriers they face in climbing the corporate ladder.

Summary and Conclusion

In Chapter 5, a review of the four previous chapters, and the interpretation of findings in relation to literature was provided. Also presented was the significance of the study findings, limitations of the study, implications of findings, recommendations for future actions, recommendations for future research studies pertaining to barriers experienced by immigrants in the United States, and summary and conclusion.

Recommendations for organizational leaders and Kenyan immigrants were made for future research and exploration. Recommendations for Kenyan immigrants in mid to senior management roles included acknowledging the themes that resulted from the current study. Participants' experiences were organized into relevant themes namely; networking, social environment, leadership process, culture, economic environment, organization politics, and discrimination. These themes supported the study findings and recommendations.

Recommendations for future actions offered effective leadership behaviors and practices to improve the chances of Kenyan immigrants to pursue and attain leadership positions in their organizations. The recommendations were categorized as social networking, developing leadership model, leadership styles, organizational change, and managing diversity.

Future studies were recommended to duplicate the study in another geographical location offering a different demographic of the study participant, or through the use of other theoretical frameworks, to explore studies focusing on different elements outside the scope of this current research that have a direct impact on career development for immigrants in private or public organizations.

References

Abdul, Q. C., & Javed, H. (2012). Impact of transactional and laissez faire leadership style on motivation. *International Journal of Business and Social Science, 3*(7). Retrieved from http://search.proquest.com/docview/1010404396?accountid=458

Adar K., & Munyae I., (2001). Human rights abuse in Kenya under Daniel Arap Moi, 1978-2001. *African Studies Quarterly, 5*(1), 1-17. Retrieved from: www.africa.ufl.edu/asq/v5/v5i1a1.pdf

Adida, C., D. Laitin, and M.-A. Valfort (2010). Identifying Barriers to Muslim Integration in France. *Proceedings of the National Academy of Sciences of the United States of America 107*(52):22384–22390.

Ali, U., & Waqar, S. (2013). Teachers' organizational citizenship behavior working under different leadership styles. *Pakistan Journal of Psychological Research, 28*(2), 297-316. Retrieved from http://search.proquest.com/docview/1524244981?accountid=458

Alvesson, M., & Sandberg, J. (2011). Generating research questions through problematization. *Academy Of Management Review, 36*(2), 247-271. doi:10.5465/AMR.2011.59330882

Ande, T. A. (2009). *Academic leadership experiences of foreign-born African immigrants in American institutions of higher education* (Order No. 3374720). Available from ProQuest Dissertations & Theses Full Text. (304899746). Retrieved from http://search.proquest.com/docview/304899746?accountid=45 8

Annan, B. (2007). *West African managers in American businesses: A cross-cultural adaptation model.* Retrieved from http://search.proquest.com/docview/304706706?accountid=35 812

Arain, M., Campbell, M.J., Cooper, C.L., & Lancaster, G.A. (2010). What is a pilot or feasibility study? A review of current practice and editorial policy. *BMC Medical Research Methodology, 10, 67.*

Arnold, K. A., & Loughlin, C. (2013). Integrating transformational and participative versus directive leadership theories. *Leadership & Organization Development Journal, 34*(1), 67-84. doi:http://dx.doi.org/10.1108/01437731311289974

Arthur, J. A., (2000). I*nvisible Sojourners: African Immigrant Diaspora in the United States.* Praeger Publishers, pp. 20–26.

Arthur, J. A., (2010). *"Transnational African Immigrant Lives and Identities," African Diaspora Identities.* Lexington Books, pp. 79–87.

Avolio, B. J., &Yammarino, F. J. (2008). T*ransformational and charismatic leadership: The road ahead.* San Diego, CA: Emerald.

Bailey, C. (2006). *A guide to qualitative field research.* Thousand Oaks, CA: Pine Forge Press.

Baker, B. & Rytina, N. (2014). Estimates of the Lawful Permanent Resident Population in the United States: January 2013. *Office of Immigration Statistics, Policy Directorate, US Department of Homeland Security.* Retrieved from http://www.dhs.gov/sites/default/files/publications/ois_lpr_pe _2013_0.pdf

Bannon, A. L. (2007). Designing a constitution-drafting process: Lessons from kenya. *The Yale Law Journal, 116*(8), 1824-1872. Retrieved from http://search.proquest.com/docview/198490234?accountid=45 8

Baral, R., & Bhargava, S. (2010). Work-family enrichment as a mediator between organizational interventions for work-life balance and job outcomes. *Journal of Managerial Psychology, 25*(3), 274-300. doi:http://dx.doi.org/10.1108/02683941011023749

Barone, M. (2013). Migration Trends of the Future. Time.Com, 1.

Bass, B. M. (1985). Leadership and performance beyond expectations. New York: Free Press.

Bass, B.M. (1997). Does the transactional–transformational leadership paradigm transcend organizational and national boundaries? American Psychologist, 52 (2) (1997), pp. 130–139

Bass, J. (2003). *Business leadership.* Jossey-Bass Publishers, San Francisco.

Beck, C. T. (2009). Critiquing qualitative research. *AORN Journal, 90*(4), 543-554. doi:10.1016/j.aorn.2008.12.023

Berlin, I. (2010). Migrations Forced and Free. Smithsonian, 40(11), 80.

Bernard, H. R. (2013). *Social Research Methods: Qualitative and Quantitative Approaches.* (2nd ed.) Sage publications Inc.

Bernhardt, A., Dresser, L., & Hatton, E. (2003). The coffee pot wars: Unions and firm restructuring in the hotel industry. In E. Appelbaum, A. Bernhardt, & R. J. Murnane (Eds.), *Low wage America: How employers are reshaping opportunity in the workplace* (pp. 33-76). New York: Russell Sage Foundation.

Berry, J. W. (2003). Conceptual approaches to acculturation. Acculturation: Advances in theory, measurement, and applied research. (pp. 17-37) *American Psychological Association.* doi:http://dx.doi.org/10.1037/10472-004

Beskow, L., Check, D., Namey, E., Dame, L., Lin, L., Cooper, A., &Wolf, L. (2012). Institutional review boards' use and understanding of certificates of confidentiality. *Plos One, 7*(9), e44050. doi:10.1371/journal.pone.0044050

Bolman L. G., & Deal T.E. (2013). *Reframing Organizations: Artistry, Choice, and Leadership.* (5thed). San Francisco, CA: John Wiley & Sons, Inc.

Borah, J. (2013). The immigrant population in Northwest Alabama: Barriers and opportunities. *Journal of Community Positive Practices, 13*(3), 36-51. Retrieved from http://search.proquest.com/docview/1461719254?accountid=458

Boyd, B. (2014). Leadership That Settled the Frontier. *Journal of Leadership Education, 13*(2), 170-175. doi:10.12806/V13/I2/I1

Branch, D. (2011). *Kenya: Between hope and despair, 1963 – 2011.* Great Britain, TJ International Ltd, Padstow, Cornell.

Briggs, V. M. (2012). The elusive goal: The quest for a credible immigration policy. *Journal Of Policy Analysis & Management, 31*(4), 956-963. doi:10.1002/pam.21656

Brown, Birnstihl & Wheeler (1996). Leading without authority: An examination of the impact of transformational leadership cooperative extension work groups and teams. *Journal of Extension, 34* (5) Feature articles, 5FEA3

Bukhari, I., & Kamal, A. (2015). Relationship between perceived organizational politics and its negative outcomes: Moderating role of perceived organizational support. *Pakistan Journal of Psychological Research, 30*(2), 271-288. Retrieved from http://search.proquest.com/docview/1780135956?accountid=3 5812

Burgess, J., & Waterhouse, J. (2010). Balancing Work, Family and Life: Introduction to the Special Edition. *Australian Bulletin Of Labour, 36*(2), 130-132.

Burnard, P., & Naiyapatana, W. (2004). Culture and communication in Thai nursing: a report of an ethnographic study. *International Journal of Nursing Studies 41* (2004) 755–765

Butler, L. (2008). Networking in the 21st century - don't get left behind! Training and Development in Australia, 35(6), 25-26. Retrieved from http://search.proquest.com/docview/208559664?accountid=35 812

Cadei, E. (2015). Hey! Who left the boarder open?. *Newsweek Global, 165*(11), 20.

Caldwell, C., Dixon, R., Floyd, L., Chaudoin, J., Post, J., & Cheokas, G. (2012). Transformative Leadership: Achieving Unparalleled Excellence. *Journal of Business Ethics, 109*(2), 175-187. Doi: 10.1007/s10551-011-1116-2

Campbell, K.M., (2011). The road to S.B 1070: How Arizona became ground zero for the immigrants' rights movement and the continuing struggle for Latino civil rights in America. *Harvard Latino Review, 14*, 1-22.

Capps, R., McCabe, K., and Fix, M. (2012). Diverse Streams: African Migration to the United States, Migration Policy Institute, pp. 8–9. Retrieved from www.migrationpolicy.org/sites/default /files/publications/CBI-AfricanMigration.pdf

Casanova, J. (2007) "Immigration and the New Religious Pluralism: A European Union/United States Comparison." In Democracy and the New Religious Pluralism. Ed. T. Banchoff. New York: Oxford University Press. Pp. 59–83.

Cashman, C. S., & McCraw, P. (1993). Conducting qualitative research in instructional technology: Methods and techniques. Proceedings of selected research and development presentations at the 15th convention of the Association for Education Communications and Technology, New Orleans, LA. (ERIC Document Reproduction Service No. ED362155)

Chaudhry, A., Javed, H., & Sabir, M. (2012). The Impact of Transformational and Transactional Leadership Styles on the Motivation of Employees in Pakistan. Pakistan Economic And Social Review, 50(2), 223-231.

Chemers, M. (2002). An integrative theory of leadership. Psychology Press, Mahwah, N.J

Chenail, R. J. (2011). Interviewing the investigator: Strategies for addressing instrumentation and researcher bias concerns in qualitative research. *The Qualitative Report, 16*(1), 255-262. Retrieved from http://search.proquest.com/docview/854984835?accountid=35 812

Chen, Lee, & Barnes (2010). The Effects of Leadership Styles on Knowledge-Based Customer Relationship Management Implementation. *International Journal of Management and Marketing Research, 3*(1).

Christensen, L. B., Johnson, R. B., & Turner, L. A. (2010). *Research methods, design, and analysis* (11th ed.). Boston, MA: Allyn& Bacon.

CIA (2015). *The world fact book: Kenya.* Retrieved from https://www.cia.gov/library/publications/the-world factbook/geos/ke.html

Cilesiz, S. (2011). A phenomenological approach to experiences with technology: Current state, promise, and future directions for research. *Educational Technology, Research and Development, 59*(4), 487-510. doi:http://dx.doi.org/10.1007/s11423-010-9173-2

Cisneros, H. (2012). The importance of national efforts to integrate immigrants. *La Prensa San Diego* Retrieved from http://search.proquest.com/docview/1437941206?accountid=35812

Clarke, R. D. (2005). Workplace Bias Abounds. *Black Enterprise,* 36, 38. Retrieved from http://search.proquest.com/docview/217918157?accountid=35812

Clawson, J. G. (2006). Level three leadership: Getting below the surface (3rd ed.). Upper Saddle River, NJ: Pearson.

Conner, J. (2000). Developing the global leaders of tomorrow. Human Resource Management, 39(2), 147-157. Retrieved from http://search.proquest.com/docview/222128163?accountid=35812

Connor, P., & Koenig, M. (2013). Bridges and Barriers: Religion and Immigrant Occupational Attainment across Integration Contexts Bridges and Barriers: Religion and Immigrant Occupational Attainment across Integration Contexts. *International Migration Review, 47*(1), 3-38. doi:10.1111/imre.12012

Cope, D., (2015). Conducting pilot and feasibility studies. *Oncology Nursing Forum, 42*(2), 196-197. doi:http://dx.doi.org/10.1188/15.ONF.196-197

Cope, J. (2005). Researching entrepreneurship through phenomenological inquiry: Physical and methodical issues. *International Small Business Journal, 23*(2), 163-189.

Corner, J. (2014). The fast are eating the slow: Mentoring for leadership development as a competitive method. *Industrial and Commercial Training, 46*(1), 29-33. doi:http://dx.doi.org/10.1108/ICT-07-2013-0052

Daly, K. J. (2007). *Qualitative methods for family studies and human development.* Thousand Oaks, CA: Sage.

Davies, I. (2009). Latino Immigration and Social Change in the United States: Toward an Ethical Immigration Policy. *Journal Of Business Ethics, 88*(2), 377-391. doi:10.1007/s10551-009-0291-x

De George, R. T. (2010). *Business ethics* (7th ed.). Upper Saddle River, NJ: Prentice Hall.

De Kluyver, C. A., & Pearce ll, J. A. (2012). *Strategy: A view from the top* (4th ed.). Upper Saddle River, NJ: Pearson.

Delorenzo, J. (2015). U.S. History: Immigration & Migration. Retrieved from http://regentsprep.org/Regents/ushisgov/themes/immigration/index.htm

Dickson, M.W., Castano N., Magomaeva A., & Den Hartog D.N. (2012). Conceptualizing leadership across cultures. Journal of World Business, 47 (4), 483–492. http://dx.doi.org/10.1016/j.jwb.2012.01.002

Dorfman, P., Javidan, M., Hanges, P., Dastmalchian, A., & House, R. (2012) GLOBE: A twenty year journey into the intriguing world of culture and leadership. *Journal of World Business. 47*(4), 504–518. http://dx.doi.org/10.1016/j.jwb.2012.01.004

Drost, E. A. (2011). Validity and Reliability in Social Science Research. *Education Research and Perspectives, 38*(1), 105-123.

Duleep, H., & Regets, M. (2014). U.S. Immigration Policy at a Crossroads: Should the U.S. Continue Its Family-Friendly Policy?. *International Migration Review, 48*(3), 823-845. doi:10.1111/imre.12122

Dunbar, D. P., & Kinnersley, R. T. (2011). Mentoring female administrators toward leadership success. *Delta Kappa Gamma Bulletin, 77*(3), 17-24. Retrieved from http://search.proquest.com/docview/905838339?accountid=35812

Eisler, R., & Carter, S. (2010). *Transformative Leadership: From Domination to Partnership. Revision, 30*(3/4), 98-106. doi:10.4298/REVN.30.3.4.98-106

Foner, N., & Alba, R. (2008). Immigrant religion in the U.S. and western Europe: Bridge or barrier to inclusion? *The International Migration Review, 42*(2), 360-392. Retrieved from http://search.proquest.com/docview/215272217?accountid=458

Gambino, C.P., Trevelyan, E.N., & Fitzwater, J.T., (2014). The Foreign-Born Population From Africa: 2008–2012. Retrieved from http://www.census.gov/library/publications/2014/acs/acsbr12-16.html

Gardner, L. (2008). Memoing in qualitative research: Probing data and processes. Journal of Research in Nursing, 13(1), 76-77.

Gee, J., Loewenthal, D., & Cayne, J. (2013). Phenomenological research: The case of Empirical Phenomenological Analysis and the possibility of reverie. Counselling Psychology Review, 28(3), 52-62.

Gentry, A. N. (2009). The student leadership challenge, five practices for exemplary leaders. NACTA Journal, 53(4), 71. Retrieved from http://search.proquest.com/docview/214378238?accountid=35812

Georgi, A. (2006). Difficulties encountered in the application of the phenomenological method in the social sciences. *Analise Psicologica, 3*, 353-361.

Gibson, C., Hardy,Jay H., I.,II, & Buckley, M. R. (2014). Understanding the role of networking in organizations. *Career Development International, 19*(2), 146-161. doi:http://dx.doi.org/10.1108/CDI-09-2013-0111

Gill, P., Stewart, K., Treasure, E., & Chadwick, B. (2008). Methods of data collection in qualitative research: Interviews and focus groups. *British Dental Journal, 204*(6), 291-5.doi:http://dx.doi.org/10.1038/bdj.2008.192

Gilmore, M., & Miller, M. M. (2013). Writings of lions: Narrative inquiry of a Kenyan couple living in the U.S. *The Qualitative Report, 18*(4), 1-14. Retrieved from http://search.proquest.com/docview/1504410429?accountid=458

Giri, V. N. (2006). Culture and Communication Style. *Review Of Communication, 6*(1/2), 124-130. doi:10.1080/15358590600763391

Githongo, J. (2006). Inequality, ethnicity and the fight against corruption in Africa: A Kenyan perspective. *Economic Affairs, 26*(4), 19-23. doi:10.1111/j.1468-0270.2006.00664.x

Godwin, R. M. (2002). A critical look at Kenya's non-transition to democracy. *Journal of Third World Studies, 19*(2), 89-111. Retrieved from http://search.proquest.com/docview/233189480?accountid=458

Golafshani, N. (2003). Understanding Reliability and Validity in Qualitative Research. *The Qualitative Report, 8* (4), 597-607. Retrieved from http://www.nova.edu/ssss/QR/QR8-4/golafshani.pdf

Goodsell, C.T. (2006). A new vision for public administration. Public Administraion review, 66, 623-635.

Gordon, A., (1998). "The New Diaspora: African Immigration to the United States," *Journal of Third World Studies,* 15(1): 81–87. Retrieved from www.inmotionaame.org/texts/viewer.cfm?id=13_011T&page=79

Gotsis, G., & Kortezi, Z. (2011). Bounded self-interest: A basis for constructive organizational politics. *Management Research Review,* 34(4), 450-476. doi:http://dx.doi.org/10.1108/01409171111117889

Greenfield, B. H., & Jensen, G. M. (2010). Understanding the lived experiences of patients: Application of a phenomenological approach to ethics. *Physical Therapy,* 90(8), 1185-97. Retrieved from http://search.proquest.com/docview/743885943?accountid=458

Grieco, E. M., et al., (2010). *The Foreign-Born Population in the United States: American Community Survey Reports*, U.S. Census Bureau, May 2012, page 10, www.census.gov/prod/2012pubs/acs-19.pdf

Groenewald, T. (2004). A Phenomenological Research Design Illustrated. *International Journal of Qualitative Methods, 3*(1), 1-26.

Groves, K., & LaRocca, M. (2011). An Empirical Study of Leader Ethical Values, Transformational and Transactional Leadership, and Follower Attitudes toward Corporate Social Responsibility. *Journal of Business Ethics, 103*(4), 511-528. Doi:10.1007/s10551-011-0877-y

Hargis, M. B., Watt, J. D., & Piotrowski, C. (2011). Developing Leaders: Examining the Role of Transactional and Transformational Leadership Across Contexts Business. *Organization Development Journal, 29*(3), 51-66.

Hart, D. M. & Acs, Z. J. (2011). High-Tech Immigrant Entrepreneurship in the United States. *Economic Development Quarterly, 25*(2) 116–129. DOI: 10.1177/0891242410394336.

Haynes, J. M. (2016). Formulating a Research Question. *AARC Times, 40*(3), 18-19

Hein, S. F., & Austin, W. J. (2001). Empirical and hermeneutic approaches to phenomenological research in psychology: A comparison. *Psychological Methods, 6*(1), 3-17. doi:http://dx.doi.org/10.1037/1082-989X.6.1.3

Hirschfield, I.S., Ross, R.K., and Silard, T.P. (2013). U.S. Should Follow California's Lead on Immigration. *Philantopic, a blog of opinion and commentary.* Retrieved from http://pndblog.typepad.com/pndblog/

Hirsh, E., & Lyons, C. J. (2010). Perceiving discrimination on the job: Legal consciousness, workplace context, and the construction of race discrimination. Law & Society Review, 44(2), 269-298. Retrieved from http://search.proquest.com/docview/874023546?accountid=35812

Hornsby, C. (2013). Kenya: A history since independence. (New paperpack edition). I. B.Tauris & Company, Limited.

House, R.J., Hanges, P.J., Javidan, M., & Dorfman. P.W. (2002). Understanding cultures and implicit leadership theories across the globe: An introduction to project GLOBE. *Journal of World Business, 37* (2002), pp. 3–10

House, R.J., Hanges, P.J., Ruiz-Quintanilla, A.S., Dorfman, P.W., Javidan, M., Dickson, M et al. (1999). Cultural influences on leadership and organizations: Project GLOBE. W.H. Mobley (Ed.), Advances in global leadership, Vol. 1JAI Press, Stamford, CT (1999), pp. 171–233

Hoyt, J. (2009). "We are America": Immigrants and social capital in the United States today. *National Civic Review, 98*(1), 14-24.

Hughes, L. (2011). 'Truth be Told': Some Problems with Historical Revisionism in Kenya. *African Studies, 70*(2), 182-201. doi:10.1080/00020184.2011.594626

Hurtado-de-mendoza, A., Gonzales, F. A., Serrano, A., & Kaltman, S. (2014). Social isolation and perceived barriers to establishing social networks among Latina immigrants. *American Journal of Community Psychology, 53*(1-2), 73-82. doi:http://dx.doi.org/10.1007/s10464-013-9619-x

Hutton, E. L. (2012). *Perception of organizational openness to performing kouzes & posner's five practices of exemplary leadership.* (Order No. 3542570, Walsh College). ProQuest Dissertations and Theses, 179.Retrieved from http://search. proquest.com/docview/1151826929?accountid=458. (1151826929).

ILO, (2015). ILO Global estimates of migrant workers and migrant domestic workers : results and methodology / International Labour Office - Geneva

ILO, (2016). Labor migration: International Labour Standards on Migrant workers. Retrieved from http://www.ilo.org/global/topics/labour-migration/lang--en/index.htm

IPC (2012). African immigrations in America: a demographic overview. Retrieved from http://immigrationpolicy.org/sites/default/files/docs/african_fa

ct_sheet.pdf

Institute of International Education (2015). Sub-Saharan Africa. Retrieved from http://www.iie.org/en/Our-Global-Reach/Sub-Saharan-Africa.

Islam, T., Aamir, M., Ahmed, I., & Muhammad, S. K. (2012). The impact of transformational and transactional leadership styles on the motivation and academic performance of students at university level. *Journal of Educational and Social Research, 2*(2), 237-244. Retrieved from http://search.proquest.com/docview/1399977980?accountid=3 5812

Jaggers, J., Gabbard, W. J., & Jaggers, S. J. (2014). The Devolution of U.S. Immigration Policy: An Examination of the History and Future of Immigration Policy. *Journal Of Policy Practice, 13*(1), 3-15. doi:10.1080/15588742.2013.855695

Jimenez, T. R., (2011). Immigrants in the United States: How well are they integrating into society? Improving US and EU immigration systems. Retrieved from www.migrationpolicy.org

Jogulu, U., & Wood, G. (2007). Power struggle [staff empowerment]. *Engineering Management, 17*(3), 36-37.doi:10.1049/em:20070306

John, H. E., & Moser, H. (1989). From trait to transformation: The evolution of leadership theories. *Education, 110*(1), 115.

Johnson, K. (2014). Theories of Immigration Law (June 30, 2014). Arizona State Law Journal, Vol. 46, No. 4, 2015. Available at SSRN: http://ssrn.com/abstract=2460890

Johnson, K. R., (2011). Sweet home Alabama? Immigration and civil rights in the "new" south. *Stanford law review*, 63, 22.

Kabukuru, W. (2013). Kenya's 50 dramatic years. *African Business,* (393), 64-66.

Kahn, S. R. (2008). The leadership challenge. *Choice, 45*(7), 1203. Retrieved from http://search.proquest.com/docview/225706411?accountid=35 812

Kameny, R.R., DeRosier, M. E., Taylor, L.C., McMillen, J.S., Knowles, M.M., & Pifer, K. (2014) Barriers to Career Success for Minority Researchers in the Behavioral Sciences. *Journal of Career Development, 41*(1) 43-61

Kandel, W. A., (2014). U.S. Family-Based Immigration Policy. *Congressional Research Service Report for Congress*, 7-5700 www.crs.gov R43145. Retrieved from https://fas.org/sgp/crs/homesec/R43145.pdf

King, A.J. (2010). Follow me! I'm a leader if you; I'm a failed initiator if you don't? *Behavioural Processes*, 84, 671–674.

Kioko, M. M. (2010). *Transnational connections of first generation immigrants from Kenya in the United States* (Order No. 3418771). Available from Ethnic NewsWatch; ProQuest Central; ProQuest Dissertations & Theses Full Text. (751307918). Retrieved from http://search.proquest.com/docview/751307918?accountid=45 8

Kirkbride, P. (2006). "Developing transformational leaders: the full range leadership model in action", *Industrial and Commercial Training*, Vol. 38 Iss: 1, pp.23 – 32

Knight, K. L. (2010). Study/Experimental/Research design: Much more than statistics. *Journal of Athletic Training, 45*(1), 98-100.

Kposowa, A. J. (2002). Human capital and the performance of African immigrants in the U.S. labor market. *Western Journal of Black Studies, 26*(3), 175-183. Retrieved from http://search.proquest.com/docview/200355396?accountid=45 8

Koh, J., Goh, E., Yu, K., Cho, B., & Yang, J. (2012). Discrepancy between participants' understanding and desire to know in informed consent: are they informed about what they really want to know? *Journal Of Medical Ethics, 38*(2), 102-106. doi:10.1136/jme.2010.040972

Kouzes, J., & Posner, B. (1995). *The leadership challenge.* San Francisco, CA: Jossey-Bass.

Kouzes, J. M., & Posner, B. (1992). The Team Leadership Practices Inventory. Retrieved from http://search.ebscohost.com.ezproxy.apollolibrary.com/login.a spx?

Kouzes, J. M., & Posner, B. Z. (2001). *Leadership practices inventory* (2nd ed.). San Francisco: Jossey-Bass.

Kouzes, J. M., & Posner, B. Z. (2002). The leadership practices inventory: Theory and evidence behind the five practices of exemplary leaders. Retrieved from http://media.wiley.com/assets/463/74/lc_jb_appendix.pdf

Kouzes, J. M., & Posner, B. Z. (2003). *The five practices of exemplary leadership.* San Francisco, CA: Pfeiffer.

Kouzes, J. M., & Posner, B. Z. (2007). *The leadership challenge.* (4th ed.). San Francisco, CA: John Wiley & Sons, Inc.

Kouzes, J., & Posner, B. (2012a). A Look at Today's Challenges for Leaders. *World, 11*(3), 6-8.

Kouzes, J., & Posner, B. (2012 b). Leadership Challenge. (cover story). *Leadership Excellence, 29*(8), 3-4.

Krieger, N. (2012). Who and What Is a 'Population'? Historical Debates, Current Controversies, and Implications for Understanding 'Population Health' and Rectifying Health Inequities. *Milbank Quarterly, 90*(4), 634-681. doi:10.1111/j.1468-0009.2012.00678.x

Kusow, A. M. (2014). African immigrants in the united states: Implications for affirmative action. *Sociology Mind, 4*(1), 74-83. Retrieved from http://search.proquest.com/docview/1501428516?accountid=4 58

Lanna-Lipton, L. (2007). *The relationship between mentoring and career advancement of millennial generation women in leadership* (Unpublished doctoral dissertation). University of Phoenix, Phoenix, AZ. (UMI 3425724)

Ledarskapscentrum (2009). The full range leadership model. Retrieved from http://ledarskapscentrum.wordpress.com/2012/06/09/the-full-range-leadership-model/

Leedy, P. D., & Ormrod, J. E. (2010). *Practical research: Planning and design* (9th ed.). Upper Saddle River, NJ: Prentice Hall.

Lemay, L. (2009). The practice of collective and strategic leadership in the public sector. *The Innovative Journal: The Public Sector Innovative Journal, 14*(1), 2, 1-19.

Leonard, K. M., Vam Scotter, J. R., & Pakdil, F. (2009). Culture and Communication: Cultural Variations and Media Effectiveness. *Administration & Society 41*(7) 850–877. SAGE Publications. DOI: 10.1177/0095399709344054

Leon, A.C., Davis, L.L., & Kraemer, H.C. (2011). The role and interpretation of pilot studies in clinical research. Journal of Psychiatric Research, 45, 626-629. doi:10.1016/j.jpsychires.2010.10.008

Lipowski, E. E. (2008). Developing great research questions. American *Journal Of Health-System Pharmacy, 65*(17), 1667-1670. doi:10.2146/ajhp070276

Liu, J., Liu, X., & Zeng, X. (2011). Does transactional leadership count for team innovativeness? *Journal of Organizational Change Management, 24*(3), 282-298. doi:http://dx.doi.org/10.1108/09534811111132695

Lloyd, B. (2005),"Coaching, culture and leadership", Team Performance Management: *An International Journal,* Vol. 11 Iss 3/4 pp. 133 – 138. http://dx.doi.org/10.1108/13527590510606334

Locke, L.F., Silverman, S.J., & Spirduso, W.W. (2010). *Reading and understanding research,* 3rd Ed. Thousand Oaks: Sage Publications

Lowman, J., & Palys, T. (2007). Strict Confidentiality: An Alternative to Pre's "Limited Confidentiality" Doctrine. *Journal Of Academic Ethics, 5*(2/4), 163-177. doi:10.1007/s10805-007-9035-7

Lucas, T., Rudolph, C., Zhdanova, L., Barkho, E., & Weidner, N. (2014). Distributive Justice for Others, Collective Angst, and Support for Exclusion of Immigrants. *Political Psychology, 35*(6), 775-793. doi:10.1111/pops.12204

Malhotra, S. (2013). Framing a research question and generating a research hypothesis. I*ndian Journal of Medical Specialities, 4*(2), 325-329. doi:10.7713/ijms.2013.0031

Malos, R. (2012). Leadership Styles. *Annals Of Eftimie Murgu University Resita, Fascicle II, Economic Studies,* 421-426.

Mapp, T. (2008). Understanding phenomenology: The lived experience. *British Journal of Midwifery*, 16, 308-311.

Martin, M. T. (1999). 'Fortress Europe' and third world immigration in the post-cold war global context. *Third World Quarterly, 20*(4), 821-837. Retrieved from http://search.proquest.com/docview/219769971?accountid=35812

Marshall, C., & Rossman, G. B. (2011). *Designing qualitative research* (5th ed.). Thousand Oaks, CA: Sage.

Marshall, S. M. (2009). The student leadership challenge: Five practices for exemplary leaders. *Journal of College Student Development, 50*(2), 245-247. Retrieved from http://search.proquest.com/docview/195183725?accountid=45 8

Maxon, R., (2011). Kenya's independence constitution: constitution-making and end of empire. Maryland, Fairleigh Dickinson university press, 358pp. Retrieved from: http://dx.doi.org/10.1080/02589001.2012.664686

Maxwell, J. A. (2005). *Qualitative research design: An interactive approach* (2nd ed.). Thousand Oaks, CA: Sage Publication.

Maxwell, J. (1998). Designing a qualitative study. In L. Bickman & D. Rog (Eds.), *Handbook of applied social research methods.* Thousand Oaks, CA: Sage.

McCabe, K. (2011). African immigrants in the United States. Washington, DC: Migration Policy Institute. Retrieved from http://www.migrationpolicy.org/article/african-immigrants-united-states

McCallum, S.,Y., Forret, M.,L., & Wolff, H. (2014). Internal and external networking behavior. *Career Development International, 19*(5), 595. Retrieved from http://search.proquest.com/docview/1658152296?accountid=3 5812

Merriam, S.B. (2009). Qualitative research: A guide to design and implementation. San Francisco: Jossey-Bass.

Minkov, M., & Hofstede, G. (2011). The evolution of Hofstede's doctrine. *Cross Cultural Management, 18*(1), 10-20. doi:http://dx.doi.org/10.1108/13527601111104269

Montuori, A. (2010). Transformative Leadership for the 21st Century: Reflections on the Design of a Graduate Leadership Curriculum. *Revision, 30*(3/4), 4-14.

Moody, C. (2006). Migration and Economic Growth: A 21st Century Perspective. Migration and New Zealand and treasury working paper. Retrieved from http://www.treasury.govt.nz/publications/research-policy/wp/2006/06-02/twp06-02.pdf

Moskowitz, S. (2009). Hofstede's five dimensions of culture. In C. Wankel (Ed.), *Encyclopedia of business in today's world.* (pp. 817-819). Thousand Oaks, CA. SAGE Publications, Inc. doi: http://dx.doi.org.ezproxy.apollolibrary.com/10.4135/97814129 64289.n468

Moustakas, C. (1994). *Phenomenological research methods.* Thousand Oaks, CA: SAGE Publications, Inc. doi: http://dx.doi.org.ezproxy.apollolibrary.com/10.4135/97814129 95658

MPI, (2015). The Kenyan Diaspora in the United States. Prepared for the Rockefeller Foundation-Aspen Institute Diaspora Program (RAD). Retrieved from http://www.migrationpolicy.org/sites/default/files/publications/RAD-KenyaII.pdf

Muchiri, M., & Kiambati, K. (2015). Relating Leadership Processes, Societal Culture and Knowledge Management: A Theoretical Model. *Journal of Global Business Issues, 9*(1), 29-38.

Mueller, S. D. (2009). It's Our Turn to Eat: The Story of a Kenyan Whistle-Blower. *International Journal of African Historical Studies, 42*(2), 312.

Mueller, S. (2011) Dying to win: Elections, political violence, and institutional decay in Kenya, *Journal of Contemporary African Studies, 29*:1, 99-117, DOI:10.1080/02589001.2011.537056

Nahavandi, A. (2012). *The art and science of leadership* (6th ed.). Upper Saddle River, NJ: Pearson Prentice Hall.

Neuman, W. L. (2006). *Social research methods: Qualitative and quantitative approaches* (6th ed.). Boston, MA: Allyn & Bacon.

Neuman, W. L. (2009). *Social research methods: Qualitative and quantitative approaches* (7th ed.). Boston, MA: Allyn & Bacon.

Nielsen, M. (2013). Bullying in work groups: The impact of leadership. *Scandinavian Journal of Psychology, 54*(2), 127-136. doi:10.1111/sjop.12011

Ochieng, P. A. (2009). An analysis of the strengths and limitation of qualitative and quantitative research paradigms. Problems of education in the 21st century, volume 13.

Odera, L. A. (2007). *Acculturation, coping styles, and mental health of first generation kenyan immigrants in the united states* (Order No. 3253373). Retrieved from http://search.proquest.com/docview/304848626?accountid=458

Odle-dusseau, H., Britt, T. W., & Bobko, P. (2012). Work-family balance, well-being, and organizational outcomes: Investigating actual versus desired Work/Family time discrepancies. *Journal of Business and Psychology, 27*(3), 331-343. doi:http://dx.doi.org/10.1007/s10869-011-9246-1

Otiso, K.M., (2007). Profile of Kenyans in the US and what it means for Kenya. Retrieved from: http://www.jaluo.com/wangwach/200705/Kefa_M_Otiso0501 07.html

Palys, T., & Lowman, J. (2006). Protecting Research Confidentiality : Towards a Research-Participant Shield Law. *Canadian Journal of Law & Society/Revue Canadienne Droit Et Societe, 21*(1), 163-185.

Papa, J., & Whelan, J. (2015). Regaining the Economic Edge: Policy Proposals for High-skill Worker and Student Authorizations. *Indiana international and comparative law review, 25*(1). http://dx.doi.org/10.18060/7909.0003

Papanikitas, A. (2011). Ethicality and confidentiality: is there an inverse-care issue in general practice ethics? *Clinical Ethics, 6*(4), 186-190. doi:10.1258/ce.2011.011036

Pape, E. (2003). Stay At Home, Europe. *Newsweek (Atlantic Edition), 142*(4), 26.

Park, S. M., (2012). Toward the trusted public organization: Untangling the leadership, motivation, and trust relationship in U.S. federal agencies. *The American Review of public Adinistration. 42*(5) 562-590. doi:10.1177/0275074011410417

Pedraja-Rejas, L., Rodríguez-Ponce, E., Delgado-Almonte, M., & Rodríguez-Ponce, J. (2006). Transformational and Transactional leadership: A study of their influence in small companies. Ingeniare: *Revista Chilena De Ingenieria, 14*(2), 159-166. Retrieved from http://search.proquest.com/docview/203586437?accountid=35812.

Peri, G. (2012). *Rationalizing U.S. immigration policy: Reforms for simplicity, fairness, and economic growth.* Washington: Brookings Institution Press. Retrieved from http://search.proquest.com/docview/1530640900?accountid=458

Plascencia, L. F. B., Freeman, G. P., & Setzler, M. (2003). The decline of barriers to immigrant economic and political rights in the American states: 1977-2001. *The International Migration Review, 37*(1), 5-23. Retrieved from http://search.proquest.com/docview/215273835?accountid=458

Platow, M. J., Haslam, S. A., Reicher, S. D., & Steffens, N. K. (2015). There is no leadership if no-one follows: Why leadership is necessarily a group process. International Coaching *Psychology Review, 10*(1), 20-37.

Polkinghorne, D. E. (2005). Language and meaning: Data collection in qualitative research. Journal of Counseling *Psychology, 52*(2), 137

Popa, B. M. (2013). Risks resulting from the discrepancy between organizational culture and leadership. *Journal of Defense Resources Management, 4*(1), 179-182. Retrieved from http://search.proquest.com/docview/1372955109?accountid=458

Portes, A. (1997). Immigration Theory for a New Century: Some Problems and Opportunities. *International Migration Review, 31*(4), 799–825. http://doi.org/10.2307/2547415

QSR International, (2016). NVivo 11 Pro for Windows. Retrieved from http://www.qsrinternational.com/product/nvivo11-for-windows/pro

Raes, E., Decuyper, S., Lismont, B., Van, d. B., Kyndt, E., Demeyere, S., & Dochy, F. (2013). Facilitating team learning through transformational leadership. *Instructional Science, 41*(2), 287-305. doi:http://dx.doi.org/10.1007/s11251-012-9228

Raja, A., & Palanichamy, P. P. (2011). Leadership styles and its impact on organizational commitment. *Journal of Commerce* (22206043), 3(4), 15-23.

Ramírez Solís, E. R., Monroy, V. I. B., & Orozco-Gómez, M. (2014). The inner circle: How politics affects the organizational climate. *Journal of Organizational Culture, Communication and Conflict, 18*(1), 65-87. Retrieved from http://search.proquest.com/docview/1647822677?accountid=3 5812

Rathi, N., & Barath, M. (2013). Work-family conflict and job and family satisfaction. Equality, Diversity and Inclusion: *An International Journal, 32*(4), 438-454. doi:http://dx.doi.org/10.1108/EDI-10-2012-0092

Rocco, T.S., & Plakhotnik, M.S. (2009). Literature, reviews, conceptual frameworks, and theoretical frameworks: Terms, functions, and distinctions. *Human Resources Development Review, 8*(1), 120-130.

Rudolph, L.C., (2007). Kenyan Americans. Countries and their cultures forum. Retrieved from http://www.everyculture.com/multi/Ha-La/Kenyan-Americans.html

Rumano, M. B. (2009). The Quest for Education in a Foreign Land: Detours and Barriers Along the Paths of the Immigrant Students from Sub-Saharan Africa in the United States. *International Journal of Diversity In Organisations, Communities & Nations, 9*(1), 65-74.

Ryan, K. (2009). Mixed migratory flows - immigration. DISAM *Journal of International Security Assistance Management, 31*(1), 24-26. Retrieved from http://search.proquest.com/docview/197757435?accountid=45 8

Sessoms, R. W. (2004). *The relationship of leadership development experiences to kouzes and posner's five practices of exemplary leaders.* (Order No. 3110781, Regent University). ProQuest Dissertations and Theses, 189-189 p. Retrieved from http://search.proquest.com/docview/305058155?accountid=35 812. (305058155).

Shah, S. K. A., Iqbal, J. J., Razaq, A., Yameen, M., Sabir, S., & Khan, M. A. (2011). Influential role of culture on leadership effectiveness and organizational performance. *Information Management and Business Review, 3*(2), 127-132. Retrieved from http://search.proquest.com/docview/889971030?accountid=458

Sharan, M., B. (1998). *Qualitative Research and Case Study Applications in Education. Revised and Expanded from "Case Study Research in Education."* Jossey-Bass Publishers, San Francisco.

Shinnar, R. S., (2007). A Qualitative Examination of Mexican Immigrants' Career Development: Perceived Barriers and Motivators. *Journal of Career Development, 33* (4) 338-375. http://doi: 10.1177/0894845307300413

Shuchman, M. (2014). Researcher-participant confidentiality now a formal concept in Canadian law. Canadian Medical Association. *Journal, 186*(4), 250-251. Retrieved from http://search.proquest.com/docview/1507563517?accountid=3 5812

Silverman, D. (2010). *Qualitative Research.*(3rded.) Sage publications

Simon, M., K. (2006). *Dissertation and scholarly research. A practical guide to start and complete your dissertation, thesis, or formal research project.* Kendall/Hunt publishing company

Smith, G. S. (2013). American citizenship in the revolutionary and early national eras. Retrieved from http://visionandvalues.org/docs/citizenshipandtheamerican-cause/Smith_CVW citizenship.pdf, 343–360.

Steers, R. M., Sanchez-Runde, C., & Nardon, L. (2010). *Management across cultures: Challenges and strategies.* Cambridge New York: Cambridge University Press.

Steeves, J. (2006). Beyond democratic consolidation in Kenya: ethnicity, leadership and 'unbounded politics'. *African Identities, 4*(2), 195-211. doi:10.1080/14725840600761203

Steinberg, S., (2014). "The long view of the melting pot." *Ethnic & Racial Studies 37*, no. 5: 790-794. International Security & Counter Terrorism Reference Center, EBSCOhost (accessed December 11, 2015).

Sorensen, A. (2008). Media Review: NVivo 7. *Journal of Mixed Methods Research, 2*(1), 106-108. Retrieved from Sage Publications.

Takougang, J., & Tidjani, B. (2009). Settlement patterns and organizations among African immigrants in the United States. *Journal of Third World Studies, 26*(1), 31-40. Retrieved from http://search.proquest.com/docview/233187160?accountid=458

Teddlie, C., & Yu, F. (2007). Mixed methods sampling: A typology with examples. *Journal of Mixed Methods Research, 1*(1), 77-100. Retrieved from Emerald database. Thousand Oaks, CA: Sage.

Thabane, L., Ma, J., Chu, R., Cheng, J., Ismaila, A., Rios, L.P., . . . Goldsmith, C.H. (2010). A tutorial on pilot studies: The what, why and how. Retrieved from http://biomedcentral.com.contentproxy.phoenix.edu/content/ pdf/1471-2288-10-1.pdf

The Hofstede Center (2015). Strategy, Culture, Change. What about Kenya? Retrieved from http://geert-hofstede.com/kenya.html

Tourish, D., & Jackson, B., (2008). Guest Editorial: Communication and Leadership: An Open Invitation to Engage. *SAGE Publications, 4*(3), 219-225.

Tuohy, Cooney, Dowling, Murphy, & Sixsmith (2013). An overview of interpretive phenomenology as a research methodology. *Nurse Researcher, 20*(6), 17-20.

Tyler, M., & Petsod, D. (2003). Newcomers in the American Workplace: Improving Employment Outcomes for Low-Wage Immigrants and Refugees. Retrieved from https://www.gcir.org/publications/gcirpubs/newcomers

U.S. Census Bureau, (2014). African-Born Population in U.S. Roughly Doubled Every Decade Since 1970, Census Bureau Reports. Release Number: CB14-184. Retrieved from http://www.census.gov/newsroom/press-releases/2014/cb14-184.html

U.S. Census Bureau, (2015). The Foreign-Born Population. Retrieved from http://www.census.gov/topics/population/foreign-born/about.html

USCIS (2015). Visit the United States. Retrieved from http://www.uscis.gov/visit-united-states/visit-us

U.S. Department of Homeland Security, (2014). *Yearbook of Immigration Statistics: 2013.* Washington, D.C.: U.S. Department of Homeland Security, Office of Immigration Statistics. Retrieved from https://www.dhs.gov/sites/default/files/publications/ois_yb_2013_0.pdf

US Department of State (2015). U.S. Visas. Retrieved from http://www.travel.state.gov/content/visas/en/visit/visitor.html

Vishnevsky, T., & Beanlands, H. (2004). Qualitative Research. *Nephrology Nursing Journal, 31*(2), 234-238.

Voss, G. B. (2003). Formulating Interesting Research Questions. *Journal of The Academy of Marketing Science, 31*(3), 356-359.

Wa Githinji, M., & Holmquist, F. (2012). Reform and political impunity in Kenya: Transparency without accountability. *African Studies Review, 55*(1), 53-74. Retrieved from http://search.proquest.com/docview/1017538076?accountid=35812

Wamwara-Mbugua, L. W., & Cornwell, T. B. (2010). A Dialogical Examination of Kenyan Immigrants' Acculturation in the United States. *Journal of Immigrant & Refugee Studies, 8*(1), 32-49. doi:10.1080/15562940903379118

Wamwara-Mbugua, L. W., Cornwell, T. B., & Boller, G. (2006). Triple Acculturation: The Role of African Americans in the Consumer Acculturation of Kenyan Immigrants. *Advances In Consumer Research, 33*(1), 428.

Wan Khairuzzaman, W. I., Hussain, G., & Muhammad, A. R. (2011). Integrative framework of leadership effectiveness. *International Journal of Business and Social Science, 2*(2) Retrieved from http://search.proquest.com/docview/904526700?accountid=45 8

Willis, J. W. (2007). *Foundations of qualitative research: Interpretive and critical approaches.* Thousand Oaks, CA: Sage.

Wiles, R., Crow, G., Heath, S., & Charles, V. (2008). The Management of Confidentiality and Anonymity in Social Research. *International Journal of Social Research Methodology, 11*(5), 417-428. doi:10.1080/13645570701622231

Woodward, I. C., More, E. A., & Van der Heyden, L. (2016). "Involve": The Foundation for Fair Process Leadership Communication. *INSEAD Working Papers Collection,* (17), 1-62.

Wren, J. T. (1995). *The leader's companion: Insights on leadership through the ages.* New York: The Free Press.

Wrong, M., (2009). *It's our turn to eat. The story of a Kenyan whistle-blower.* 1st U.S. ed. Great Britain. An imprint of HarperCollins publishers.

Yakushko, O., Backhaus, A., Watson, M., Ngaruiya, K., & Gonzalez, J., (2008). Career Development Concerns of Recent Immigrants and Refugees, *Journal of Career Development, 34* (4) 362-396

Yavuz, M. (2010). Adaptation of the leadership practices inventory (LPI) to Turkish. Egitim Ve Bilim, 35(158), 143. Retrieved from http://search.proquest.com/docview/1009842051?accountid=458

Yingling, M. (2013). Conventional and Unconventional Corruption. *Duquesne Law Review, 51*(2), 263-320.

Yonghee Suh, Y., Sohyun, A., & Forest, D. (2015). Immigration, imagined communities, and collective memories of Asian American experiences: A content analysis of Asian American experiences in Virginia U.S. history textbooks. *Journal of Social Studies Research, 39*(1), 39-51. doi:10.1016/j.jssr.2014.05.002

Yu, K. (2008). Confidentiality Revisited. *Journal of Academic Ethics, 6*(2), 161-172. doi:10.1007/s10805-008-9061-0

Yukl, G.A., (2006). *Leadership in organizations* (6th ed.). Upper Saddle River, NJ: Pearson Prentice Hall

Yukl, G. (2013). *Leadership in organizations* (8th ed.). Upper Saddle River, NJ: Prentice-Hall.

Appendix A
RESEARCH INSTRUMENT

Introduction and demographic information

Date of interview: _____ Start Time: _____

Participant code: _____Age range: _____ Gender: ___ (M) ___ (F)

Background Questions

1. When did you immigrate to the United States?
2. How long have you been in Northern California?
3. What is your current position?
4. How long have you held your current position?
5. What kind of organization are you employed with?

Interview Questions

1. What does being a Kenyan immigrant mean to you?
2. Please describe your experience in migrating from Kenya to the United States?
3. What is your current role in your organization?
4. In general, do you feel a sense of commitment as being part of this organization?
5. Please describe your feelings about the leadership process in your organization?
6. Please describe how you feel about the culture in your organization?
7. How are cultural issues affecting your ability in attaining leadership positions in your organization?
8. Please describe how you feel about the social environment in your organization?
9. How is the social environment affecting your chances of attaining leadership positions in your organization?
10. Please describe how you feel about the politics in your organization?

11. Do you feel that the political environment is affecting your ability in attaining leadership positions in your organization?
12. Please describe how you feel about the economic environment in your organization?
13. Do you feel that the economic environment is affecting your chances of attaining leadership positions in your organization?
14. What else would you like to share in regard to barriers faced in attaining leadership positions in your organization?
15. Before we conclude this interview, what else would you like to share about your experiences in working in the United States as a Kenyan immigrant?

End time:_____

THANK YOU FOR YOUR TIME

Appendix B
CONFIDENTIALITY STATEMENT

Project Title:

Exploring barriers Kenyan immigrants face in attaining leadership positions in Northern California: A Phenomenological Study.

John O. Mobegi

CONFIDENTIALITY STATEMENT

As a researcher working on the above research study at the University of Phoenix, I understand that I must maintain the confidentiality of all information concerning all research participants as required by law. Only the University of Phoenix's Institutional Review Board may have access to this information. "Confidential Information" of participants includes but is not limited to: names, characters, or other identifying information, questionnaire scores, ratings, incidental comments, other information accrued either directly or indirectly through contact with any participant, and/or any other information that by its nature would be considered confidential. In order to maintain the confidentiality of the information, I hereby agree to refrain from discussing or disclosing any confidential information regarding research participants to any individual who is not part of the above research study or in need of the information for the expressed purposes on the research program. This includes having a conversation regarding the research project or its participants in a place where such a discussion might be overheard: or discussing any Confidential Information in a way that would allow an unauthorized person to associate (either correctly or incorrectly) an identity with such information. I further agree to store research records whether paper, electronic or otherwise in a secure locked location under my direct control or with appropriate safeguards. I hereby further agree that if I have to use the services of a third party to assist in the research study, who will potentially have access to any Confidential Information of participants, that I will enter into an agreement with the said third party prior to using any of the services, which shall provide at a minimum the confidential obligations set forth herein. I agree that I will immediately report any known or suspected breach of this confidentiality statement regarding the above research project to the University of Phoenix, Institutional Review Board.

_____

Signature of researcher

_____

Printed Name

_____

Date

Appendix C:
INFORMED CONSENT FORM
PARTICIPANTS 18 YEARS OF AGE AND OLDER

Project Title:

Exploring barriers Kenyan immigrants face in attaining leadership positions in Northern California: A Phenomenological Study.

Dear Participant,

My name is _____ and I am a third year student at the University of Phoenix working on a Doctor of Management in Organizational Leadership degree. I am conducting a research study entitled: Exploring barriers Kenyan immigrants face in attaining leadership positions in Northern California. The purpose of this qualitative phenomenological research study is to explore the lived experiences and perceptions of Kenyan immigrants in mid to senior management positions to better understand barriers impeding promotion opportunities to leadership positions in Northern California.

Participation in this study will involve face-to-face interview, notes will be taken, and with your permission, it will be recorded using an audio recorder. The information from the recorded interview may be transcribed, and you have the option of reviewing interview transcripts for accuracy. The interview will be conducted at your convenience and at a place mutually agreed upon. The interview session will last approximately 45 to 60 minutes.

Your participation in this study is voluntary. If you choose not to participate or to withdraw from the study at any time, you can do so without penalty or loss of benefit to yourself. The results of the research study may be published, but your identity will remain confidential and your name will not be disclosed to any outside party. To maintain anonymity, I will structure a coding process to assure that your name is protected and all observations and questionnaires will be coded with a number, not your name. A record of the number that is assigned to you will be kept in a bank safety deposit box for a period of three years then destroyed.

There are no foreseeable risks to you in this research study. Although there may be no direct benefit to you, a possible benefit of your participation is to understand the lived experience and perception of barriers Kenyan immigrants face in attaining leadership positions in their organizations. If you have any questions concerning the research study, please call me at _____ or send me an email at: _____.

As a participant in this study, you should understand the following:

1. You may decline to participate or withdraw from participation at any time without consequences.

2. Your identity will be kept confidential.

3. _____, the researcher, has thoroughly explained the parameters of the research study and all of your questions and concerns have been addressed.

4. The interview will be recorded, and you grant permission for the researcher, _____, to digitally record the interview. You understand that the information from the recorded interview may be transcribed. The researcher, _____, will structure a coding process to assure that anonymity of your name is protected.

5. Data will be stored in a secure bank safety deposit box. The data will be held for a period of three years, and then destroyed.

6. The research results may be used for publication.

By signing this form you acknowledge that you understand the nature of the study, the potential risks to you as a participant, and the means by which your identity will be kept confidential. Your signature on this form also indicates that you are 21 years old or older and that you give your permission to voluntarily serve as a participant in the study described.

Signature of the participant _____ Date _____

Signature of the researcher _____ Date _____

Appendix D:
REQUEST FOR PARTICIPATION

Address of the researcher

_____

_____

Date _____

Dear (Participant's Name),

RE: REQUEST TO PARTICIPATE IN A DOCTORAL RESEARCH STUDY

My name is _____ and I am a third year student at the University of Phoenix working on a Doctor of Management in Organizational Leadership degree. I am conducting a research study entitled, 'Exploring barriers Kenyan immigrants face in attaining leadership positions in Northern California'. The purpose of this qualitative phenomenological research study is to explore the lived experiences and perceptions of Kenyan immigrants in mid to senior management positions to better understand barriers impeding promotion opportunities to leadership positions in Northern California.

This letter is to request you to be one of my purposively selected participants for the study. In order to be eligible to participate in this study, an individual would be holding mid to senior management position in their respective organization. Participation in this study will involve face-to-face interviews, and with your permission, notes will be taken and/or recorded using an audio recorder. The interview will be conducted at your convenience and at a private and secure place that is mutually agreed upon. The interview session is expected to be completed between 45 to 60 minutes.

Your participation in this study is voluntary. To maintain anonymity, each participant in the study will be assigned a code. The purpose of this is to ensure that no personal identifying information is requested from you or passed on to an outside party. If you choose not to participate in or to withdraw from the study at any time, you could do so without penalty or loss of benefit to yourself. The results of the research study would be published, but again, no identifying information will be disclosed to any outside party. Your participation in this research study will not pose direct or in-direct risks to you. Please feel free to return the enclosed page to indicate that you accept or decline to participate in this study.

Should you have any further questions, please do not hesitate to contact me through email at _____ or by phone at _____. I look forward to hear-ing from you soon. Thank you.

Yours Sincerely,

_____

Appendix E:
PREMISES, RECRUITMENT AND
NAME (PRN) USE PERMISSION

(organization name)

Name of Facility, Organization, University, Institution, or Association

Please complete the following by check marking any permissions listed here that you approve, and please provide your signature, title, date, and organizational information below. If you have any questions or concerns about this research study, please contact the University of Phoenix Institutional Review Board via email at IRB@phoenix.edu.

▶ I hereby authorize _____, a researcher from University of Phoenix, to use the premises (facility identified above and address below) to conduct a study entitled: Exploring barriers Kenyan immigrants face in attaining leadership positions in Northern California.

▶ I hereby authorize _____ , a researcher from University of Phoenix, to recruit subjects for participation to conduct a study entitled: Exploring barriers Kenyan immigrants face in attaining leadership positions in Northern California, at the facility identified above.

▶ I hereby authorize _____, a researcher from University of Phoenix, to use the name of the facility, organization, university, institution, or association identified above when publishing results from the study entitled: Exploring barriers Kenyan immigrants face in attaining leadership positions in Northern California.

Signature_____Date _____

Name _____Title _____

Email Address _____

_____

Address of Facility
(include URL if Website)

Appendix F
PINTERVIEW PROTOCOL

To ensure that participants are asked all the same questions, the interview protocol in appendix F will be used. To carry out the interviews I plan to:

1. Mail or hand over the consent form to participants and obtain consent for the study.
2. Schedule participant interviews and discuss informed consent, confidentiality, and recording of the interview.
3. Arrive 15 minutes early at the interview location.
4. Respectfully and professionally greet each interview participant and briefly introduce myself.
5. Gather written consent form from participant and begin interviews.
6. Record each interview session and indicate time, date, and participant code.
7. Begin the conversation by introducing interview questions.
8. Summarize main themes to confirm accuracy of the interview responses.
9. Conclude interview session and answer any potential questions from the participant.
10. Press stop on the recorder, and graciously thank the participant for taking part in the interview.

Appendix F
PARTICIPANT TITLES AND CODES

Participant Titles	Participant Code
District Manager	1a
Sr. Manager	2a
Project Manager	3a
Distribution Manager	4a
Operations Supervisor	5a
Customer Support Manager	6a
Senior Research Scientist	7a
Clinical Supervisor	8a
Accounting Supervisor	9a
Lead Network Engineer	10a
Director of Revenue	11a
Office Manager	12a
Senior Manager SEC	13a
Communications Director	14a
House Manager	15a
Financial Manager	16a
Corporate Controller	17a
Senior Director	18a
Site Manager	19a
Senior IT Manager	20a

Dr. John Onuko Mobegi was born and raised in Kenya and migrated to the United States after completing high school. Currently, a resident of San Jose Northern California, the heart of silicon valley, Dr. Mobegi has been an Information and Communications Technology professional for over 13 years. Dr. Mobegi has held several positions in various organizations that includes customer service, technical support and IT asset management.

Dr. Mobegi's research interests focus on the fields of management and leadership as they apply to organizations and academic disciplines, including information technology, business administration, and organizational leadership. His interest stems from the need to understand the importance and role of leadership in achieving organizational goals. The rapidly changing environments calls for transformational leaders in order to succeed in tomorrow's environment.

Dr. Mobegi holds a Bachelor of Science degree in management, Master's degree in management of information systems, and a Doctorate in Management in Organizational Leadership.

School of Advanced Studies
University of Phoenix

American Journal of
Transformational Leadership